JOB DESCRIPTIONS AND DUTIES FOR CHURCH WORKERS AND MEMBERS

by

Herbert W. Byrne, Ed.D.

Copyright © 2005 by Herbert W. Byrne, Ed.D.

Job Descriptions and Duties For Church Workers and Members
by Herbert W. Byrne, Ed.D.

Printed in the United States of America

ISBN 1-59467-252-0

All rights reserved solely by the author. The author guarantees all contents are original and do not infringe upon the legal rights of any other person or work. No part of this book may be reproduced in any form without the permission of the author. The views expressed in this book are not necessarily those of the publisher.

Unless otherwise indicated, Bible quotations are taken from the New King James Version. Copyright © 1982 by Thomas Nelson, Inc.

www.xulonpress.com

Author of

A Christian Approach to Education
Education and Divine Revelation
The Gospel of the Canaan Journey
Reclaiming Inactive Church Members

Dedication

To four boys in my life:

My son Bert,
My grandson Sean,
And my great-grandsons Connor and Chase

To a great faculty secretary,
Harriet Cook

PREFACE

This material was produced around the general theme of outlining the duties and responsibilities of Christian people who live for and serve God. It takes the form of a manual to provide guidance in Christian living and service.

The content is divided into two parts: (1) duties of church and Sunday School workers, and (2) suggestions for the development of Christian character and conduct.

A Biblical study of the duties of Christians was produced to guide and encourage Christian people in daily living. It is important for professing Christian people to know explicitly what is required of them in order to please God and live a successful and fruitful Christian life.

An attempt was made to stick closely to the Biblical texts, drawing primarily from the New Testament. To achieve maximum benefits from this work, readers and students should study passages of Scripture on each point. The King James Version was utilized because of its familiarity and preference by many who love the Bible.

Sections One through Seven reveal a suggested design for a Job Description Manual, outlining duties and responsibilities of workers. Section Eight provides the reader with a Biblical study of the duties of all Christians in their personal lives, their conduct and social situations.

TABLE OF CONTENTS

Section One
GENERAL ORIENTATION

	Page
Introduction – Purpose and Use of Manual	1
Parson to Person – Message from the Pastor	2
Message from the Chairman of the Board of Christian Education	3
Message from the Director of Christian Education	4
Chart – Organization of the Church	5
Church Calendar	6
Standards for Church Workers	8
General Requirements for All Church Workers	9
Some Practical Goals for Church Workers	9
Some Values and Advantages of Job Descriptions	10
Outline for a Job Analysis	11
Pictures of Staff and Church Facilities	13

Section Two
CONGREGATIONAL RESPONSIBILITIES AND DUTIES

Duties of the Church Membership	14
Duties of the Official Board and Chairman	15
Church Committees (Evangelism, Missions, Stewardship, Social Concerns, Worship, Pastor-Parish, Finance, Trustees, Nominations and Personnel, Leadership Training, Curriculum, Other Committees, Ad Hoc)	16
The Board of Christian Education	20
Duties of the Chairman and Officers of the Board of Christian Education	21

Section Three
GENERAL OFFICERS OF THE CHURCH AND CHURCH SCHOOL

The Pastor	23
Associate Pastors	26
Church Secretary	27
Director of Christian Education	28
General Superintendent	33
Associate Superintendents	37
Church School Secretary	38
Church School Treasurer	39
Church Administrator or Business Manager	39
Registrar	39
Literature Secretary	41
Secretary of Technology	41
Church Librarian	41
Committee on Church School Administration	42
Worship Chairman of the Children's Department	43

Section Four
WORKERS IN THE SUNDAY CHURCH SCHOOL

Common Responsibilities and Duties of Superintendents............................	44
General Duties of the Division Superintendents..	44
Superintendents of the Children's Departments and Regulations	45
Children's Division Regulations	46
Superintendent of the Youth Division	48
Superintendent of the Adult Division..	49
Department Superintendents...	50
Duties of General Departmental Workers (Associate Superintendent, Department Secretary, Pianist, Chorister, Librarian, Associates)....................	53
Cradle Roll Superintendent and Workers	55
Nursery Department Superintendent and Workers......................................	57
Beginner (Kindergarten) Department Superintendent and Workers...............	58
Primary Department Superintendent and Workers......................................	59
Junior Department Superintendent and Workers	60
Middle School Department Superintendent and Workers	60
High School Department Superintendent and Workers...............................	61
Adult and College Age Department Superintendents and Workers...............	62
Home and Extension Department Superintendent and Workers...................	63
Class Officers and Workers...	64

Section Five
TEACHERS IN THE SUNDAY CHURCH SCHOOL

Personal Qualifications of the Teacher...	66
Duties and Responsibilities of Teachers...	68
Nursery Teacher Responsibilities..	73
Beginner (Kindergarten) Teacher Responsibilities..	74
Primary (Elementary 1, 2, 3) Teacher Responsibilities....................................	75
Junior (Elementary 4, 5) Teacher Responsibilities...	76
Middle School (6, 7, 8) Teacher Responsibilities...	77
High School (9, 10, 11, 12) Teacher Responsibilities......................................	77
College Age Teacher Responsibilities..	78
Adult Teacher Responsibilities...	78

Section Six
WORKERS IN OTHER CHURCH AGENCIES

Superintendent of Weekday Kindergarten Program.....................................	80
Responsibilities of Youth Fellowship Leader or Sponsor.................................	80
Scout Leader...	80
Institutional Representative for Boy Scouts...	81
Institutional Representative for Girl Scouts..	81
Vacation Bible School Director..	82
Conference Christian Education Director for the Denomination......................	83
Youth Director or Educational Assistant for Youth	84
Junior or Children's Church Director..	87
Men's and Women's Organization Workers..	87
Music Workers (Director, Song Leaders, Choir Directors, Choir Members).........	87

Superintendent of Transportation and Outreach...............................	89
Transportation and Outreach Workers..	89
Director or Superintendent of Training..	91
Recruiting Questionnaire..	92

Section Seven
OTHER SUGGESTIONS FOR THE MANUAL

Supplies and Services..	95
Use and Care of Rooms and Facilities	95
How to Order Supplies	95
Church School Fact Sheet	96
Workers' Conference	97
Workers' Banquet	97
Open House	97
Promotion Sunday	97
Other Suggestions for the Manual..	97
Workers' Conference Calendar...	98
The Secret of Successful Service...	99

Section Eight
THE DUTIES OF CHRISTIANS

The Priority of Obedience...	100
The Duty to Deity	104
Personal and Individual Duties...	108
The Believer's Walk..	129
Sacred and Religious Responsibilities...	131
Ministerial Responsibilities...	137
Social Duties..	141

SECTION ONE

GENERAL ORIENTATION*

*It is suggested that the manual for each local church include such introductory matters which will orient workers and prospective workers to the general nature of the local church and its program. Some statement regarding the nature of the manual itself would be helpful, particularly to new workers. This is why a section entitled General Orientation has been included herewith.

INTRODUCTION

Purpose of the Manual

The purpose and objectives of all functions in the local church are to qualify men and women to reveal and glorify God, exalt Christ, live by the leading of the Holy Spirit, and serve God and our fellowmen.

No matter how well-organized a Sunday School or church may be, the success will depend upon those who administer its plans and policies and teach in the school. The failure of administration, supervision and teaching in so many churches and church schools is often due to the unfitness of the workers. It is important, therefore, that all workers be carefully chosen, and, as far as practicable, well trained for their tasks.

All workers in the program of the local church need to know exactly and specifically what their duties are. A very practical tool, devised to help bring this about, is the job description. Leaders and administrators in the business world have long seen the value of such an instrument and have used it extensively with their employees. Likewise, many churches are finding that job descriptions and listings of duties help volunteer workers to understand just what is expected of them.

A job description is simply a written explanation of a responsibility to be performed by the church worker, describing the nature of the job and the duties involved in functioning in the capacity demanded. While it is recognized that most of the tasks of the church worker across the country are similar in nature, a job description will allow for some flexibility in, and adjustment of, duties to meet local demands. In a very real sense, therefore, job descriptions can be "tailor-made" for individual situations.

Church leaders who see the need for job descriptions and work toward the adoption of some form of this practice will find for themselves how practical, helpful and fruitful they can be when used properly. It is to this end that this manual is dedicated, with the hope that it will motivate and guide God's people to do a more efficient work of building His kingdom.

Use of This Manual

The job descriptions listed are illustrative in character. It is recommended that they be used as guidelines in the formulation of descriptions to be used in any particular church situation. Each church should work out carefully for itself statements on each job called for in its program solely on the basis of local demands and commitments.

It is recommended that a special Committee on Personnel be appointed whose responsibility it will be to study the local church situation in terms of what and how many jobs are required to run its program; then describe each one of these jobs in a manual of the type here illustrated.

A MESSAGE FROM THE PASTOR- Parson to Person
(Sample)

Centuries ago a man addressed Jesus with these words, "Master, we know that you are a teacher sent from God, for no man can do the things you are doing unless God is with him." This sentence, spoken to the greatest Teacher of all history, expresses the philosophy of this church regarding your task as a worker in the church. We want you to feel that you have been "sent from God," called and commissioned by Him for the job you have undertaken. This means that your work is being done for Him, not merely to fill a vacancy in the church. It also means that, since every other worker has been called of God, you will realize that you are on a divine team and will, therefore, view your particular task, not one of isolation, but as one part of a coordinated plan for leading people to Christ.

However, merely the "feeling" of a divine mission is not, by itself, enough. Did you ever stop to realize that for every year of work Christ had spent ten years of preparation! To carry out your "calling" will require a lot of careful planning and disciplined preparation so that you will be "filled with the Holy Spirit and wisdom." This is a day of the "knowledge explosion," and we expect you to meet this with a working and relevant knowledge of the Word of God. Our staff will work with you, and we will expect you to work with them in constantly finding better ways and means of communicating the Good News. We will expect you to attend meetings and workshops which will help you to be the best possible worker.

There is a comfort as well as a challenge in the verse above, which we have quoted, for it also says, "No one can do these things unless God is with him." It is wonderful to know that God not only sends us out as workers but also goes with us. The "Go teach" is accompanied by the "Lo—I am with you always." This means that the greatest Teacher of all times will be with you as you do your work. Surely, then we cannot fail!

Your Pastor (fill in name)

MESSAGE FROM THE CHAIRMAN OF THE BOARD OF CHRISTIAN EDUCATION
(May be called SS Council, Commission on Education, etc.)
(Sample)

This handbook has been prepared for workers, leaders and teachers in the program of our local church. You are the key leaders and persons in the church who have the knowledge and understanding and provide the initiative and inspiration for the planning and executing of the Christian Education program. The strength and effectiveness of the teaching ministry of our church will largely depend upon your dedication to this task. Together you have a common concern and compulsion for sharing the good news of Christ with children, youth and adults. Indeed, you have been commissioned by your church in the name of Christ to teach God's Word and share God's love not only to the household of faith but also to those outside. The words of the Master ring in our ears: "Go therefore....teaching them to observe all that I have commanded you."

> How can we teach them more effectively?
> How can we reach them?
> How can we win them?
> How can we train them for service?

This handbook helps us to lay out responsibilities and duties which will contribute to the answers to the questions above.

Paul tells us in 2 Timothy 2:15, "Study to show thyself approved unto God, a workman which needeth not to be ashamed; rightly dividing the word of truth." This verse impresses us with three things: (1) the necessity of being approved of God for His work; (2) the need for quality in serving Him; and (3) the necessity to exercise skill in getting the job done. By a clear knowledge of what we are supposed to do, we will come nearer to the realization of these things than in any other way. It is to this task that this book is dedicated.

Chairman of the Board of Christian Education. (Fill in name)

Slogans

"To fail to plan is to plan to fail "

"Plan your work; then work your plan"

"The only circumstance where success
comes ahead of work is in the dictionary"

MESSAGE FROM THE DIRECTOR OF CHRISTIAN EDUCATION
(Also known as Minister of Christian Education or Supervisor)
(Sample)

Welcome to the staff of the church and church school of _____ church. You can look forward to many happy and fruitful hours of service to Christ, His church, and to His precious children. You will have the satisfaction of knowing that what you do and what you say in your classes and places of responsibility will help form the Christian character of the next generation. Therefore, it is our prayer that God may continually give you an abundant measure of His Holy Spirit to perform this vital part of the Christian ministry which we all share.

Many of us have questions when we enter into an important task, even those with many years of experience. This manual, therefore, has been prepared to help answer your questions and help you become better acquainted with our church, church school program and policies. Please read through the manual carefully, underlining as you go, and, if you have any questions or suggestions, let us know. We earnestly pray that your experience in all the programs of the church will be richly rewarding for you and for all whom you serve in the Master's name.

Please call on us as your fellow worker and helpmates in all of the work that God has called us to do. I am at your service.

Your Director of Christian Education (Fill in name)

ORGANIZATION OF THE CHURCH

Each church should create a flow chart to show how the church is structured and organized. Such a chart should be revised annually.

CHURCH CALENDAR

You will, of course, not want to adopt all the suggestions for the annual calendar below, but they will serve as a guide.

October
1. Conduct Rally Day
2. Conduct Missionary Day
3. Celebrate Columbus Day
4. Hold World Temperance Sunday
5. Celebrate Halloween
6. Recognize United Nations Day
7. Hold Layman's Day
8. Celebrate National Bible Week
9. Emphasize an enlargement program
10. Promote December items
11. Promote Thanksgiving plans
12. Check on Sunday School for the past year
13. Begin the Sunday School year
14. Hold Monthly workers' conference

November
1. Celebrate Armistice Day
2. Celebrate Thanksgiving Day
3. Conduct Missionary Sunday
4. Conduct Decision Day
5. Celebrate All Saints Day
6. Emphasize Bible Study
7. Promote Christmas plans
8. Plan for workers' training class or weekly training class
9. Hold monthly workers' conference
10. Take Census
11. Hold Father-Son Banquet

December
1. Celebrate Universal Bible Sunday
2. Celebrate Christmas Day
3. Conduct Missionary Sunday
4. Make training plans
5. Hold Monthly workers' conference

January
1. Commemorate Epiphany Sunday
2. Conduct Missionary Sunday
3. Celebrate Universal Week of Prayer
4. Celebrate New Year's Day
5. Hold Monthly workers' conference
6. Celebrate Youth Week

February
1. Conduct World Day of Prayer
2. Celebrate Boy Scout Sunday
3. Celebrate Lincoln's Birthday
4. Celebrate Washington's Birthday
5. Celebrate Valentine's Day
6. Celebrate National Freedom Day
7. Hold National Crime Prevention Week
8. Conduct planning activities
9. Conduct Missionary Sunday
10. Celebrate National Smile Week
11. Hold Monthly workers' conference
12. Promote March plans

March
1. Celebrate Palm Sunday
2. Conduct Missionary Sunday
3. Conduct Loyalty campaign to follow-up Easter
4. Hold Monthly workers' conference
5. Conduct School of Missions
6. Promote for April plans
7. Plan for May events

April
1. Celebrate Easter Sunday
2. Celebrate Arbor Day
3. Celebrate National Baby Week
4. Conduct Loyalty Campaign
5. Plan for Daily VBS
6. Plan for Children's Day
7. Plan for Father's Day
8. Honor graduates
9. Commemorate Good Friday
10. Conduct Missionary Sunday
11. Hold Monthly workers' conference

May
1. Celebrate May Day
2. Celebrate National Family Week
3. Celebrate "I Am An American" Day
4. Conduct National Day of Prayer
5. Celebrate Pentecost Sunday
6. Celebrate Memorial Day
7. Promote Summer Camps
8. Promote Daily Vacation Bible School
9. Conduct Missionary Sunday
10. Celebrate Mother's Day
11. Hold Mother-Daughter Banquet
12. Hold Monthly workers' conference

June
1. Celebrate Flag Day
2. Celebrate Children's Day
3. Conduct DVBS
4. Celebrate Father's Day
5. Hold Decision Sunday
6. Promote youth camps
7. Conduct Missionary Sunday
8. Hold Monthly workers' conference

July
1. Celebrate Independence Day
2. Conduct Missionary Sunday
3. Plan for new year
4. Plan to attract vacationers
5. Hold Monthly workers' conference
6. Hold Summer leadership classes
7. Hold Sunday School picnic

August
1. Celebrate Friendship Day
2. Celebrate Homecoming Sunday
3. Conduct Missionary Sunday
4. Plan for Promotion Day
5. Plan for Installation Day
6. Plan for Rally Day
7. Plan for enlargement
8. Get vacationers back
9. Hold Monthly workers' conference
10. Conduct Summer leadership training

September
1. Celebrate Labor Day
2. Conduct Missionary Sunday
3. Honor Robert Raikes' birthday (14th)
4. Celebrate Religious Education Week
5. Conduct Promotion Day
6. Conduct Installation Day
7. Plan for Rally Day
8. Plan for enlargement
9. Hold Monthly workers' conference
10. Start an attendance crusade
11. Hold Workers' retreat to plan New Year's work

It is further suggested that a theme for each month be adopted. This theme shall prove to be the guiding factor in setting the pace of the promotional emphasis for that particular month. A year's program can be planned if your workers give time to a retreat in the fall of each year during which the program will be definitely planned.

STANDARDS FOR CHURCH WORKERS

1. A good worker has a personal encounter with Jesus Christ, resulting in a regenerate Christian life; a personal daily walk with Christ.

2. A good worker believes in the Bible as the inspired Word of God.

3. A good worker will be motivated by the love of God, to reveal Christ, and to be led by the Holy Spirit in his daily life.

4. A good worker is a radiant growing Christian and a loyal supporter of the church program.

5. A good worker lives in his daily life those Christian moral and ethical principles he seeks to impart to others. (See the Duties of Christians in Section Eight)

6. A good worker attends the Sunday worship services and Sunday School regularly; in case of absence, he notifies his superintendent, or class president, in time to permit substitute help to be provided.

7. A good worker is an evangelist who believes in the Word of God, is earnest in prayer, and is interested in the spiritual welfare of others.

8. A good worker is a friend who knows his pupils, plays with them occasionally, visits in their homes, and tries to understand their needs.

9. A good worker studies his lesson sufficiently to adequately interpret the Scriptures for the needs of the pupils.

10. A good worker reads books and magazines pertaining to his work and attends Leadership Training Schools whenever available.

11. A good worker cultivates his own personality in order that he may be an attractive, happy and pleasant person.

12. A good worker develops self-discipline and self-control that he may accept the responsibility of leading others.

13. A good worker keeps adequate records and is prompt to carry out assignments.

2 Timothy 2:15

"Study to show thyself approved unto God, a workman that needeth not to be ashamed; rightly dividing the word of truth."

GENERAL REQUIREMENTS FOR ALL CHURCH WORKERS

1. They shall be loyal and faithful to the overall program of the church for which they work.

2. They shall be conscientious and trustworthy in fulfilling all duties with which they are entrusted.

3. All workers, unless their jobs specifically designate so, shall be at the church 10-15 minutes before starting time; any later arrival will be considered late.

4. All business shall be conducted in a Christian manner.

5. All workers should be faithful in their attendance at the services of the church, including church school, Sunday morning services, evening services, and midweek prayer meetings.

6. All efforts of the workers, it should be remembered, are to the glory of God and should glorify and magnify His name.

SOME PRACTICAL GOALS FOR CHURCH WORKERS

1. To know Christ personally and to introduce Him to others

2. To learn the contents of the Bible and to convey this knowledge to others

3. To learn and present the claims of Christ

4. To provide oneself with a systematic plan of Bible study and to help others find a plan of study

5. To learn the doctrines of the Christian faith

6. To learn how to use Scripture to help one face daily life

7. To learn to face problems that are relevant to today's needs; to help others with the same needs

8. To learn the skills of Christian communication

SOME VALUES AND ADVANTAGES OF JOB DESCRIPTIONS

1. To help church congregations practice the functional principle of Christian service – seeing areas of service responsibilities and carrying out the duties in such areas

2. To help leaders perform the functions of planning, organizing, executing, supervising, co-coordinating, publicizing, and evaluating the work to be done

3. To assist in the implementation of the program that is planned

4. To clarify the needs for good organization by clearly identifying the positions and jobs to be filled

5. To stress the importance of depth, thus contributing to supervision by listing duties to be performed

6. To contribute to co-ordination and smooth functioning of personnel by indicating the relationship of one position to another and clearly identifying the place of such jobs

7. To test and measure both progress and quality of work attempted by providing a basis for evaluation

8. To generate a feeling of confidence and security on the job by giving each worker a sense of direction

OUTLINE FOR A JOB ANALYSIS
(Teacher, Administrator, Director, or Supervisor)

Purpose: to serve as a guide in creating one's own job description manual

A. SCOPE AND OBJECTIVES OF THE PROGRAM
1. For what type of job is the worker needed? Is it a single or combined job such as teacher, supervisor, director, consultant, director-teacher, supervisor-teacher, or director-supervisor? Define the type of position for which the person is employed.

2. What type of person is needed for this job? Describe the type of person in terms of personality and character, education, and experience.

3. Working conditions
    a. What is the salary and plan of salary increase?
    b. What is the length of the term of employment?
    c. What provisions are made for social security, insurance, annuity, etc.?
    d. What is the plan for vacation, sick leave, and substitute teachers? (Usually follows local public school practice)
    e. How many classes and pupils will the teacher have? What grades will he/she teach? What will be the size of the classes? What will be the length of the class periods?
    f. What provision is made for duplication needs and supplies, equipment, transportation, and necessary expenses?
    g. What kind of contract will you have with the worker; formal or informal (letter)?

B. RESPONSIBILITIES RELATED TO THE TEACHING
1. What daily preparation is expected?
2. Which of the following activities will be expected to be done: Bible study, worship, service projects, creative activities, or other experiences?
3. How much time and attention shall he/she give to individual pupil guidance? What arrangements are made for a time for personal counseling?
4. What home contacts should the teacher make? Should he/she do home visitation, consultation, reports, letters, etc.?
5. What church contacts should the teacher make? To what extent should he/she visit the churches of the pupils, report denomination preferences to churches, or confer with church officials concerning pupils and program?
6. In what forms of in-service training will the teacher be expected to engage? What assistance will the administrative council provide?
7. Will you provide opportunity for teachers to attend state and national Christian Education conferences by providing substitutes, transportation, and part of the expenses?
8. In what ways will he/she be expected to cooperate with the administrator and the governing board? What regular conferences will he be expected to attend? What records and reports will he/she be asked to make?

C. RESPONSIBILITIES RELATED TO ADMINISTRATION
1. What are the responsibilities of the worker in planning for housing, including arrangements for:
   a. Heat and janitorial services?
   b. Equipment?
   c. Other supplies (visuals, etc.)?
2. What are his/her duties in enrolling pupils?
3. What is his/her part in working out schedules for teachers and pupils?
4. With whom and to what extent does he/she work in building, evaluating, and revising the curriculum ?
5. To what extent and with whom does he/she plan the budget?
6. To what extent will he/she be responsible for promoting and publicizing the program?
7. What will be his/her specific responsibility in employing and directing the personnel?
8. To whom should his/her regular reports be made?
9. What provision for secretarial help is given?
10. What shall be his duties in relationship to
    a. Churches of the community?
    b. Other faiths?
    c. Homes?
    d. Public school?
    e. Other community agencies?

D. RESPONSIBILITIES RELATED TO SUPERVISION
1. What are his/her responsibilities in explaining the purpose and nature of the curriculum?
2. What are his/her duties in evaluating and improving the quality of teaching?
3. How much time will be given in his/her schedule to the study and improvement of working conditions?
   a. Of the pupils – such as attractive rooms, teacher attitudes, etc.?
   b. Of the teachers – such as a sense of personal security?
4. How much of his/her time should be given to personal conferences with teachers, guiding their reading, planning the curriculum, and setting up general conferences?
5. To what extent will he/she be encouraged and enabled to attend state and national conferences?

E. OTHER RESPONSIBILITIES
What other responsibilities will this worker have? Define them clearly.

PICTURES OF STAFF AND CHURCH FACILITIES

At this point in your Manual, it is suggested that you place selected pictures of your ministerial staff, church school workers, and church and Sunday School facilities.

SECTION TWO

DUTIES OF THE CHURCH MEMBERSHIP

1. To recognize Christian Education as one of the great ministries of God and the church

2. To make provision for the support of the program of Christian Education as a part of the total church program

3. To set up goals for all segments and departments in the church program

4. To make provision for the practice of the five great program elements of the church: evangelism, worship, fellowship, instruction, and service

5. To operate according to the best principles of organization, administration and supervision

6. To build and work the program according to the following program characteristics: grading, variety, unity, comprehensiveness, flexibility, simplicity, practicality, and spirituality

7. To organize the program to achieve optimum efficiency

8. To administrate the program to achieve optimum effectiveness

9. To supervise the program to achieve maximum results

10. To finance the program to provide adequate support

11. To publicize the work to draw maximum response

12. To periodically evaluate the program to determine progress

13. To involve every member in service activities

14. To pray for vision, power, results and the leadership of the Holy Spirit

15. To strive to glorify God in all efforts and activities

DUTIES OF THE OFFICIAL BOARD* AND CHAIRMAN
*Also known as Administrative Council, Board of Elders, etc.

Purpose: to initiate planning, receive reports, set goals, authorize action, determine policy, evaluate the church's ministries, and review the state of the church

Meetings: monthly, but at least quarterly. Special meetings may be called by the chairman, pastor, or members of the Board

Responsibilities

The Board shall:

1. Administer the organization of the local church, including structure, officers, committees and workers

2. Determine the fiscal year and tenure of office of all workers unless specifically limited otherwise

3. Establish goals for the church, elect officers and workers according to church rules, receive reports and review the state of the church

4. Encourage the support of the missions program and any of the benevolences decided upon

5. Make proper and adequate provision for the financial needs of the church

6. Discharge faithfully any and all duties and responsibilities committed to it by the congregation and law of the church

7. Develop in the members of the congregation a concern and responsibility for the establishment of new churches and other forms of ministry needed in the community

8. Foster understanding of the unity of the church and encourage cooperation with other Christian bodies and agencies

Chairman

1. He shall preside over the Board.

2. He shall work with the pastor to see that all responsibilities of the Board are fulfilled as listed under the responsibilities and duties of the Board.

CHURCH COMMITTEES*(WITH CHAIRMEN)

Evangelism Committee

1. Obtain guidance materials for and study the implications of evangelism for the total mission of the church
2. Interpret and recommend to the official Board goals and ways of implementing the mission of the church represented by the work of evangelism, including membership care
3. Make specific recommendations of the work of evangelism for different age groups in the church and for reaching all people in the community
4. Serve as liaison within and beyond the local church

Missions Committee

1. Inform the official Board of the purposes and needs of programs and institutions supported in the nation and around the world
2. Provide study resources for different age groups in keeping with the standards and guidance of the denomination
3. Survey the needs of the local community and recommend to the official Board plans for local mission and service projects
4. Inform the church of the qualifications and needs for personnel to serve through the church around the world
5. Develop a benevolence budget and submit it to the official Board and/or the finance committee
6. Represent the concerns of missions within and beyond the local church

Stewardship Committee

1. Contact church agencies and obtain guidance materials for stewardship and study the implications for the total mission of the church
2. Keep the church membership and the official Board aware of the meaning of the stewardship of life, time, talents, and materials, interpreting and recommending ways of implementing the mission of the church through stewardship
3. Make specific recommendations on stewardship for various age groups
4. Recommend to the official Board other materials and methods for inspiring people to be involved in service and mission in keeping with the standards and guidance of the denomination

Each congregation will decide on what and how many committees to have.
The following are suggestive of possibilities:

Social Concerns Committee

1. Keep the official Board and membership aware of the need for study and action in areas of peace and world order, human relations, political and economic affairs and general welfare
2. In keeping with the standards and guidance of the denomination, recommend to the official Board and membership study-action projects in the field of social concerns
3. Make recommendations to the various age groups for work in this area
4. Cooperate with other church agencies in surveying the needs of the local community and in recommendations for local social-action projects

Worship Committee

1. Help the congregation to become increasingly aware of the meaning, purpose and practice of worship
2. In keeping with the standards set up by the denomination, recommend plans for study by both individuals and groups on the act of worship, with specific recommendations for different age groups
3. Cooperate with the pastor in caring for music, ushering, furnishings, appointments and sacramental elements for congregational worship
4. Recommend standards for placement in the church of memorial gifts as aids to worship

Committee on Pastor-Parish Relations

The primary function of this committee is to aid the pastor in making his ministry effective by keeping him advised concerning the conditions and needs of the congregation. They should be alert to the status of relations between the pastor and people and interpret to the people the nature and function of the pastoral office.

1. Cultivate pastor-parish relationships
2. With full knowledge of all concerned, meet with various church officials to consult on pastor-parish relationships
3. After consultation with the pastor, recommend to the official Board people to fill other professional and lay staff positions created by the Board
4. Where there is a multiple staff, relate to the entire staff
5. When there is a need for a change of pastors, confer with the pastor and other church officials to help bring about a proper settlement

Committee on Finance

1. Receive all financial requests to be included in the annual budget of the church
2. Compile annually a complete budget for the local church and submit to the official Board for review and adoption
3. After approval of the budget by the official Board, develop and implement plans which will raise sufficient income to meet the adopted budget

4. Administer the funds received according to instructions from the official Board
5. Provide for an annual audit of the records of the financial officers of the local church and all its organizations and shall report to the congregation

Trustees

1. The trustees may incorporate the local church, if directed by the congregation, expressly subject to the law of the denomination and local laws that will fully protect and exempt the individual officials and members from any and all legal liability
2. The congregation may direct the trustees with respect to the purchase, sale, mortgage, encumbrance, construction, repairing, remodeling, and maintenance of any and all property of the local church
3. The congregation may direct the trustees with respect to the acceptance or rejection of any and all conveyances, grants, gifts, donations, legacies, bequests, or devises, absolute or in trust, for the use and benefit of the local church, and require the administration thereof and of the local laws appertaining thereto
4. The congregation may do any and all things necessary to exercise such other powers and duties relating to the property, real and personal, of the local church concerning as may be committed to it by the law of the church

Committee on Nominations and Personnel

1. Nominate for appointment and election such officers and members of boards and committees as the law of the church requires
2. Serve throughout the year to guide the official Board on personnel matters to coordinate the leadership and service needs with the personnel of the congregation

Committee on Leadership Training

This committee on leadership training shall assist the pastor, the official Board, and General Superintendent in the following activities:

1. Develop and conduct periodic leadership training schools for all parts of the educational program of the local church
2. Provide a regular flow of training and resource materials to church school workers
3. Develop and conduct a special orientation program as needed for new workers
4. Identify potential leaders in the church membership and recommend to the Board of Christian Education their placement in appropriate jobs in the church and its educational program

Committee on Curriculum, Educational Materials, and Library

This committee shall be composed of a chairman, librarian, pastor, general superintendent, secretary of literature, department superintendents, and two appointed members at large. Their responsibilities are these:

1. Assist the General Superintendent, the Board of Christian Education, and departmental workers in the determination and implementation of the educational program curriculum
2. Recommend adequate resource literature and other educational materials which complement current and planned study programs
3. Solicit materials for the church library and arrange for the staffing of this facility
4. Establish and maintain an adequate equipment and materials inventory for the educational program

Other Committees, Agencies, Groups and Offices

1. Deacons
2. Elders
3. Lay Leaders
4. Lay Members
5. Men's Organizations
6. Women's Organizations
7. Committee on Health and Welfare
8. Committee on Public Relations
9. Committee on Good Literature
10. Committee on Ecumenical Affairs
11. Church Administrators (Business Manager)
12. Church Treasurer
13. Financial Secretary
14. Membership Secretary
15. Secretary of Enlistment

Provision for Ad Hoc Committees and Groups

The need arises periodically for special committees and groups to be formed to deal with areas of concern and developmental tasks. For the most part, these groups will deal with specific problems, discharge their responsibility, and be released. These groups may have representation from within the membership of the congregation as well as outside the membership. Task Force Groups may be formed from time to time specifically for the purpose of considering outreach of the church.

THE BOARD OF CHRISTIAN EDUCATION*

May also be known as Sunday School Council, Commission on Education, Christian Education Committee, etc.

Duties

1. To organize, manage, and supervise all educational activities in the Sunday School, weekday schools and organizations
2. To coordinate the work of various organizations and committees
3. To see that the total program of education is properly organized
4. To study the educational needs of the church
5. To provide for all necessary meetings of various committees and organizations in the program
6. To provide for the proper observance of special days
7. To see that adequate supervision is made available to all divisions of the church school
8. To keep the members of the congregation informed on the needs, progress, and program of the church school
9. To see that special education on the evils of beverage alcohol, tobacco, and promotion of race relations, world peace, community service, etc., is given to the congregation
10. To encourage cooperation in community matters and interdenominational projects
11. To constantly review the curriculum and counsel with workers on materials and methods
12. To allocate space for departments, classes, and other groups and to study the needs for facilities
13. To provide a library for leadership needs
14. To select and elect officers and teachers for the church school
15. To set up and administer a program of leadership education
16. To provide guidance for youth in Christian vocations and in Christian service
17. To create throughout the church school both an attitude and a program of evangelism and to cooperate in the total church program of evangelism
18. To cooperate in the church program of missions, to cultivate the missionary spirit in all divisions, and to provide a definite missionary curriculum in all age groups
19. To constantly seek to increase enrollment and attendance and also to make careful provision for an absentee follow-up program
20. To plan carefully for a budgetary system of finances in the church school
21. To constantly evaluate the total program to determine if needs are being met and standards are being maintained
22. To ensure that all pupils are taught the Christian use of money, promoting the tithe as a minimum of giving
23. To carefully make provision for a definite program of training in Christian service in all divisions of the church school
24. To provide for a program of Christian family education and careful home-church cooperation, planning also for various family activities in the church program
25. To assist the pastor and various administrative officers in making decisions
26. To arrange for keeping accurate records and permanent records and to make them available where needed
27. To create a program calendar of the year's activities in all divisions of the church school

28. To arrange for church representation in all phases of Christian outside the local church
29. To make careful reports of its work to the official Board and to see that others make regular reports
30. To modernize all procedures and techniques as far as possible
31. To meet regularly for the study and discussion of the educational needs and problems of the congregation
32. To consider and act upon proposed changes in the program
33. To execute resolutions and policies handed to it by the official Board
34. To set standards and qualifications for the leadership of the church school
35. To adopt a "Standard of Excellence of Achievement" for the church school
36. To give particular attention to the work and needs of the Sunday School teacher
37. To constantly study its own work, duties and responsibilities
38. To give careful attention to the interpretation of music in the church, to the quality of music, to its ministry, and to the training of the pupils in all divisions
39. To provide opportunities for youth initiative
40. To inform the people about the denominational programs of Christian Education. Including schools and colleges
41. To determine various time schedules for the educational program, such as beginning and closing times, and dates for special events, etc.
42. To see that all officers and workers are installed in their positions
43. To plan and supervise the work of all schools in the total church program, such as VBS, weekday religious education, etc.
44. To create and administer the policies for directing the total church program of education in the church

Duties of the Chairman and Officers of the Board of Christian Education

Chairman of the Board of Christian Education

1. Prepare the agendas for the board
2. Consult with the pastor and the general superintendent concerning church school policies
3. Preside at the meetings of the board
4. Fulfill all obligations involved as a member of the official Board, since he is, by virtue of his job a member
5. Designate responsibility to members of the board as the needs present themselves
6. Make recommendations and suggestions to the church on the Christian education program of the church
7. Help in securing the major officers who are needed for the Christian education program of the church
8. Guide any evaluative studies and efforts made in the program of Christian education in the church
9. Report to the official Board concerning the church school work of the board
10. Report annually to the Church conference on the work of the board
11. Not take upon himself administrative responsibilities which are the job of other elected officials beneath him
12. Be vitally involved in encouraging the members of the board to carry out its purpose
13. Bring back to the board any recommendations from the official Board

14. Notify all members through the secretary as to the time and place of coming meetings
15. Strive for a close working relationship between himself and the general officers – the pastor, the general superintendent, and the division chairmen
16. Conduct board meetings as follows (an agenda): devotions, minutes, reports of officers, unfinished business, reports of superintendents of departments, new business, and department meetings
17. On Sunday be present and on time, make announcements, welcome people, and assist the superintendents

Vice Chairman

1. Preside in the absence of the chairman
2. Provide suggestions for the agenda
3. Attend regular meetings
4. Assume an individual responsibility as a member of the board

Secretary

1. Be regular and punctual in attendance
2. Consult with chairman on agenda for meetings
3. Notify all members of all meetings
4. Keep accurate minutes
5. Notify church secretary about bulletin notices
6. Take care of any correspondence required
7. Attend meetings of workers' conferences

Members

1. Attend meetings regularly; be cooperative; keep well-informed on the program
2. Develop habit of long-range planning; study strong and weak points of the program
3. Study the needs of each age group; make the total program adequate and well-balanced
4. Accept assignments cheerfully

SECTION THREE

GENERAL OFFICERS OF THE CHURCH AND CHURCH SCHOOL*

*It is recognized that the titles and presence of general officers in church and Sunday School work vary widely with the denomination represented. Following is a representative list of such officers.

Duties of the Pastor

As a Leader and General Helper

1. Interpret the privilege and task of church education to the congregation
2. Visualize the church program as a whole and organize it as a unit
3. Vitalize the major educational agencies within the congregation
4. Procure, train, and inspire leaders
5. Participate directly as necessary in strategic places in the program
6. Know Sunday School work
7. Attend Sunday School as regularly as possible
8. Work with the Board of Christian Education and the General Superintendent in formulating and directing the policies of the school
9. Avoid taking over the work of the General Superintendent
10. Be the spiritual and inspirational head of the Sunday School
11. Stand by the officers and teachers on the staff, assisting, encouraging, correcting, supporting and equipping them for the task
12. See that the work of the Sunday School is done and done well
13. Work closely with all the general officers
14. Inspire staff and congregation by keeping the educational work of the church before the Official Board and congregation
15. Make an effort to develop the "spirit" of Christian Education
16. From the pulpit show the meaning of Christian Education for the home
17. Make pastoral calls on the workers to help, encourage, and inspire them
18. Suggest good reading materials, books, etc., to all the workers
19. Use the bulletin boards, posters, newspapers, and announcements to show progress in the educational work of the church
20. Make an attempt to create a "mind to work" among the people
21. Challenge the people regarding the opportunities in Christian service
22. Occasionally preach on the call to service
23. Keep the principle of gradation before the people and workers
24. Constantly emphasize the necessity of adequate support financially
25. Take the workers to conventions, institutes, and special seminars

As an Administrator

1. Give general oversight and supervision to the educational program, but do not supersede the General Superintendent in his work as administrator
2. Keep good objectives before the staff and the standards high
3. If there is none, see that a Board of Christian Education is organized
4. Take a strong hand in finding a qualified person for General Superintendent
5. Encourage the creation and maintenance of the departments in the work of the

church school with department superintendents to assist the general superintendent in administering the work of various departments
6. See that overlapping and neglect in certain areas of the work are overcome
7. Be alert in making provisions for the various schools in a good program, such as Vacation Bible School, school of evangelism, etc.
8. In close cooperation with the Board and the General Superintendent, be responsible to see that proper and adequate buildings and equipment are provided; study facilities while in use and while empty
9. Work as a team with the Board, the General Superintendent, and the Director of Christian Education
10. See that a Manual of Procedures is made available which will list duties and responsibilities

As a Program Builder

1. Take the lead in the development of a coordinated and well-balanced program
2. Critically analyze the denominational program and make careful adaptation to it in the local church
3. Plan ahead under the leadership of the Holy Spirit
4. Help the Board and all others concerned to wisely, carefully, and prayerfully develop a calendar of activities for the year
5. Make plans for conducting an annual retreat of workers to plan the year's work and calendar

As Director of Leadership Education and Development

1. See that all workers and teachers have a genuine Christian experience and evangelical theology
2. Be constantly on the lookout for prospective teachers and workers
3. Be constantly alert to all possible service opportunities
4. Do not be averse to becoming superintendent or director of a leadership training department in the church
5. Help the Board of Christian Education and the General Superintendent formulate objectives for the program of leadership training as follows:
    a. To see what we need leaders for, where they can serve, and why
    b. To discover the right kind of leaders
    c. To enlist leaders and stress a divine call to service
    d. To train leaders, both initially and through a continuous program of growth
    e. To ensure a continuous resupply of leaders
6. Help the Board determine the leaders that are needed by listing all possible jobs and duties
7. Help the Board locate leaders through prayer and a leadership census
8. Preach occasionally on the "Stewardship of Time and Talents"
9. Help a Committee on Personnel enlist and recruit workers
10. Help the Board and operate the program of leadership training
11. Create and publish a calendar of leadership training opportunities
12. Conduct an annual installation service for all workers

As a Supervisor

1. Be an "overseer" of the entire program and work closely with the Director of Christian Education who is the principal supervisor
2. Work with people as they are and seek to make them better as workers
3. Try to get all workers to see the need for improvement; then lead them in a specific plan for improvement
4. In all this work, be a friendly helper, not a "snooping spy"
5. Try to work within your group, not as a dictator over them
6. Help in the setting up of spiritual objectives and adequate standards of procedure
7. Help all workers to make evaluations, discover weaknesses and suggest sufficient remedies
8. As time allows, work with the teachers in assisting them to improve the teaching-learning process
9. Be on the alert constantly to keep a good spirit of morale in the staff
10. Work constantly on the improvement of human relationships in the work
11. Evaluate often how well people are able to work together
12. Make plans for improving the curriculum, classroom instruction, worship, social and recreational life, and service training opportunities

As a Pulpiteer

1. Stress the importance of Christian Education
2. Inform the people, promote and advertise the program
3. Preach to meet the needs of the people
4. Demonstrate the proper use of the Bible and correct interpretation
5. Promote Christian family life
6. Stress the importance of prayer and devotional life
7. Preach great doctrines
8. Apply the principles of the gospel to everyday life
9. Train the people in the art of worship
10. Cultivate strong financial support

As a Children's Worker

1. Get acquainted with children, be their pastor and their friend; talk to them; play with them
2. Be sure a vacation Bible school is provided and take part in it
3. See that the children are provided with adequate and attractive facilities
4. Give assistance to parents and teachers who work with children
5. Set a good example for them in life and ministry
6. See that good curriculum materials and recreational equipment are provided
7. Train children in worship
8. Visit children's classes
9. Promote weekday religious education

As a Youth Worker

1. Be the friendly counselor of youth
2. Show an interest in the school and social life of youth
3. Stand by youth in time of trouble
4. Use youth in the church program, in choirs, as ushers, etc.
5. Attend classes and youth meetings
6. Help youth with the Bible
7. Give youth vocational guidance
8. Challenge youth to Christian service
9. Guide youth in church projects
10. Give youth leadership education and training
11. Preach to youth at home, in church, and at Commencement and Baccalaureate
12. Promote camps and conference for youth

As an Adult Worker

1. Provide leadership education for adults
2. Give adults guidance in Christian service activities
3. Point out social responsibilities and relationships to adults
4. Guide adults in Bible study and interpretation
5. Instruct adults in Christian ethics
6. Give adults wholesome social life and recreation
7. Challenge adults with a world-wide vision for mission
8. Lead adults to a greater appreciation and love for the church
9. Set up a Christian family life program
10. Give particular attention to young adults
11. Provide special study courses, church projects, and Christian literature for adults

Duties of Associate Pastors and Ministers

Duties vary widely here, depending on the size of the church. Such workers will not only serve as "fill-in people" for any absent ministers, but will also be assigned specific responsibilities and duties of their own. Care should be taken here to avoid misunderstanding and overlap in such work. Clearly defined areas of work should be set up with common understanding regarding limits of responsibilities so that confusion can be avoided. Illustrations of specific areas of responsibility would include assignments to be in charge of visitation, age-group work, music, etc.

Duties of the Church Secretary
(The General of the church Army)

Duties in the Church Office

1. Answer the phone and direct calls
2. Make appointments for the pastor
3. Take care of all mailings
4. Work on the computer as needed
5. Create the weekly bulletin
7. Organize and distribute office and church supplies
8. Serve as secretary of boards and committees
9. Contact general denominational organizations
10. Cooperate with the city on community matters
11. Cooperate with church organizations to meet their requests
12. Refer requests of needs to the church staff
13. Coordinate church activities and departments
14. Care for incidentals
15. Care for advertising church activities

Duties to the Pastor

1. Make appointments
2. Care for mailings
3. Typing (as needed)
4. Answer phone calls
5. Prepare agendas for board and committee meetings
6. Report sick people and all emergencies
7. Help with budgetary matters

Duties to the Congregation

1. Prepare newsletters
2. Prepare announcements and handouts
3. Answer questions
4. Make phone calls
5. Plan a Care Ministry for the community
6. Relay reports of church plans and activities
7. Refer personal and group needs to the pastor and others
8. Help solve any problems which might arise
9. Handle E-mails that come and go
10. Receive suggestions from the congregation on church improvement
11. Announce denominational and church activities
12. Organize bulletin boards and place any announcements on them

Job Analysis for the Director of Christian Education*
*Also known as Minister of Education or Educational Worker or Assistant

A. General Statement
    The Director of Christian Education, as leader and teacher of the Christian Education and mission, is responsible for interpreting and providing resources and leadership in the educational mission of the church in cooperation with the minister. The Director is responsible to the Pastoral Relations and Personnel Committee. She/he is also responsible to the minister who, as a spiritual leader and appointed elder of the Church, has the responsibility of helping to coordinate all aspects of the church mission.

B. The Director or Educational Assistant

    1. Spiritual Effectiveness
        The Director shall assist in developing a balanced educational mission- spiritually effective and educationally sound. In the pursuance of this, in addition to the accredited educational requirements, it is most essential that the Director should, first and foremost, have a vital Christian experience in his own life that will be the basis of leading others into a growing Christian experience. We would want our Director to have a sense of mission; a vision of what the overall church education process and mission can become under dedicated and trained leadership; a love for people and ability to work with them; a friendliness and tact, yet be aggressive and resourceful in carrying on his work; one of a growing maturity who will continue to grow both educationally and spiritually.
    2. Interpreter
        The Director is the interpreter of the Christian Educational mission and process as it undergirds and is a part of the total mission of the church. He should be able to see the mission as a whole and analyze the significance of all church activities and the part education can play in their outreach and achievements.
    3. Scope
        The Director should be interested in the development or growth of children, youth and adults, and assist in planning church activities which will minister to all age groups, realizing that the educational process involves the total life and mission of the church.
    4. Leadership Education and Development
        To teach, inspire and train leaders in mission are among the most important duties of the Director. These duties involve spending adequate time in counseling and coaching workers, (teachers, youth counselors, leaders, etc.), interpreting the meaning and method of Christian Education, interpreting resources and lesson materials, explaining how they are to be used, and then helping the leaders to evaluate their own work.
    5. Enlistment
        The Director shall assist in discovering and enlisting teachers and workers in cooperation with all who are concerned with the church school and others.

6. Visitation by Teachers
   The Director will encourage teachers, in the development of a person and family-centered relationship and outreach, to visit within the home for educational purposes, where so much can be done in the areas of interpretation, enlistment, and commitment.
7. Director – Minister Relationships
   In this the minister will need to share and be a team-participant. He will need, in fulfilling this, to be informed about all that is going on and be a participant in policy-making decisions as they affect the church. On the other hand, the minister will free the Director to do his job as effectively and creatively as he can, and at the same time give him understanding support. Each should see the other as a responsible minister fulfilling his unique role in the total ministry of the church.

C. Commission on Education
   1. Policies, Organization and Recommendations
      The Director is to provide guidance to the Commission on Education in determining policies for the organizing and administering of the educational program. Counsel and reports on the strengths and weaknesses of the educational process, recommendations for improvements and future plans shall be shared with the Commission, as well as with the minister and any other needed supervisory personnel.
   2. Resource Person and Counselor
      The Director is to serve as a resource person and counselor to the Church School Superintendent, the divisional superintendents (coordinators), officers, teachers, lay leader, committee chairmen, youth council, and workers in all phases of the educational program as it relates to all of the church's mission, including, for example, the work area commissions, the Women's Society of Christian Service, and also help to interpret the responsibilities of leaders and officials of the church.
   3. Finance
      The Director should counsel with the Commission on Education in preparing an adequate annual budget and give careful consideration to expenditures.
   4. Vacation Church School
      The Director should offer counsel to the vacation church school director in choosing curriculum materials, setting up the program, and enlisting and training workers.
   5. Educational Staff
      The educational staff, officers and teachers are to seek the aid and counsel of the Director in the total program of Christian Education.

D. Church School
   I. Coordinating Superintendents
      The Director is to counsel with divisional coordinators (and the church school Superintendents) in planning, supervising, and coordinating the work of the Children's Division, the Youth Division, and the Adult Division of the church school, and meet with these groups also in their regularly scheduled meetings – Departmental, workers' conferences, etc. One feature of the planning in these groups should be considering and evaluating needs, recommending policies, planning for increased attendance, ordering materials, consideration for teachers,

monitoring the spiritual commitment of the teachers and leaders as a whole, and working out arrangements and schedules in the operation of the class sessions.

2. Supervision of Workers

The Director, in cooperation with the chairman of the Education Commission and Church School Superintendent, is responsible for the pre-service and in-service training of workers. This involves counseling with individual teachers, classroom assistance, and offering guidance in the ordering and use of curriculum materials and in the method of teaching as well as evaluation of results. (Conference laboratory and demonstration schools are suggested from time to time as a further aid for training.)

3. Youth Councils

The Director will work in consultation with youth and adult councils in planning and giving supervision to the youth program of the church, including the activities both within the local church and outside the local church such as retreats, institutes, rallies, camps, etc.

4. Workers' Conference

The Director will participate in the planning of regular workers' conferences and department meetings and give general direction, guidance and supervision to over-all church school activities including observance of special days and occasions of the church year, social events, etc. An annual calendar of monthly themes will be planned and published.

5. Library

The Director will give supervision to a library committee in the selection and arrangement of good books for a church library and its use.

6. Annual Planning

The Director will encourage an Annual Retreat devoted to planning the Christian Education year. This should issue in a calendar of activities.

E. Meetings

1. Attendance

The Director is expected to attend staff meetings, Administrative Board and Council of Ministry meetings, meetings of the Commission on Education, and meetings of other commissions as needed or directed by the minister.

2. Reports

The Director is to report regularly to the Administrative Board, the Council on Ministries and the Commission on Education, and annually to the Charge Conference.

3. Outside Activities

Regarding outside activities, the Director is encouraged to participate in District and Conference activities in so far as these activities do not interfere with responsibilities at the church. The Director may serve as a counselor in the summer camping program at least one week each summer. It is desirable that the Director attend conferences and workshops which will be considered in-service training. The Director is expected to attend special conferences on Christian Education.

F. Music
   The Director is to be a consultant to the Music Director so that music in worship and music in Christian Education will be properly coordinated with the understanding that music is an integral part of the church's educational and worship ministry.

G. Salary, Vacations, and Conferences
   1. Salary
      a. first year – A.B. degree_____
      b. first year - M.R.E, degree_____
      c. Doctor's degree_____
   2. Housing
   3. Travel or car allowance
   4. An office with secretarial help
   5. Social security and hospitalization
   6. Vacation– two weeks (first) along with 2 or 3 additional days at certain times of the year, such as Christmas
   7. In-service training, workshops or conferences
   8. Sick leave
   9. Weekly schedule – one day of rest per week
      The Director is not expected to have overlong work days. Since many meetings will be held at night, it should be understood that that the Director may come in at various times of the day and maintain a flexible schedule; however, there should be scheduled, published hours when he will normally be at the church so that others may contact him. He will have one day off each week.

H. Other
   1. Governance
      The Director is to comply with the law of the church.
   2. Membership classes
      The Director is to share with the minister in planning, recruiting for and teaching the junior and youth membership classes.
   3. Publicity
      The Director will share the services of the church secretary with other members of the church staff.
   4. Home Calls
      As a future responsibility, with time permitting, the Director will spend time in making home calls – especially calls related to the educational work of the church. Calls might include homes where children and youth have been ill or absent for an extended period of time; homes of teachers and members of the educational staff, homes of families unhappy with the church school, and calls to enlist workers or for purposes of teacher consultation.
   5. Other functions
      In sharing with the minister, these functions may be performed by the Director: assisting in worship services, helping to recruit persons for Christian discipleship and uniting with the mission of the church by profession of faith or transfer of letter; leading special projects, especially as this relates to forms of ministry in the neighborhood where the church is located; encouraging the regular experience of worship on the part of those who are teaching or leading in all areas of church mission, and helping to develop

among the people of the congregation a lively sense of their vital individual and corporate ministry in the neighborhood and the world.

I. Areas Without Responsibility
In order to clarify the functions of the Director, it is wise to list some of the functions which are the responsibilities of others and should not be carried out by the Director.
1. The Director should not be a regular teacher or substitute teacher, except if he occasionally wishes to teach a class for guidance or background purposes.
2. The Director is not expected to do any of the work which is the responsibility of the church secretaries. This means that the church school secretary is primarily responsible for keeping and maintaining the attendance records; the treasurer and financial secretary are responsible for paying bills and making church school budget reports; the general church secretary and secretarial staff are responsible for duplicating, typing and other important execution of material that may have been initially prepared by the Director.
3. The Director should not be expected to secure teachers for the church school on his own. Although he will give leadership here and help with the calling, the primary responsibility comes under the superintendents and the Commission on Education.

J. Summary
In summary, it is obvious that a job description cannot include the countless details of daily procedure, of personal counseling and relationships with people, or of the leadership given to the church fellowship so that together all will participate and grow in Christ's mission in the world. This is not a rigid operational manual.

Rather, this job description seeks to provide some of the ways and means in fulfilling the heart of the work and ministry of the Director of Education in the life of a spiritually sensitive staff and people, working cooperatively in a Christ-like spirit with all members of the congregation in helping to fulfill creatively God's will in our time.

This leadership includes, of course, various areas of work in the church as it fulfills its total ministry as a "gathered, worshipping, caring community" and as a scattered "being" and "doing" mission.

It is necessary that the congregation be aware that the Director will be working in a dynamic, creative and growing relationship with others as he carries out these responsibilities. The details and specifics follow as he contributes a life of competence and devotion to people and to the Gospel in our time.
This is a tentative job analysis and is subject to review and discussion each year and/or any time upon the desire of the pastor and/or the Director, as the understanding of the educational mission of the church is broadened.

Duties of the General Superintendent

As an Organizer

1. He shall be responsible for the total activities of the children, youth and adult divisions of the church school.
2. The General Superintendent's directives should be carried out by the department superintendents, associates, teachers, workers and officers.
3. The General Superintendent, with the aid of the total staff and workers, should carry out the total program of the Sunday School.
4. He needs to see the relationship of the various parts of the program to the whole.
5. He should see that the graded principle is practiced in all departments.

As an Administrator

1. Work with the pastor, the Board, and DCE in planning the total educational program
2. Help coordinate the activities of various groups and departments
3. Promote the interests of good Christian Education in all effective ways
4. Organize a Committee on Administration or Executive Committee to coordinate the work of the officers in carrying out routine business matters
5. Direct the work of the Department Superintendents
6. Maintain regular conferences of officers and teachers
7. With the teachers, assist in making provision for housing and equipment
8. Help adopt a program of finance for the school, including stewardship
9. Set up standards for the school in collaboration with the officers and workers
10. Work for unity, enthusiasm and an atmosphere of spirituality
11. Where used, set up a schedule of worship programs
12. Keep the Sunday School positively evangelistic, doctrinally sound, and aggressively missionary
13. Be chairman of the Workers' Conference, where used
14. Stress the importance of and guide in efforts for enlargement and expansion
15. Assist in creating a master calendar of the year's program and activities
16. Help decide upon which special days to include in the calendar
17. Serve as executive of the Board of Christian Education by bringing to it matters which require its consideration, and by carrying out in turn the decisions of the Board
18. Help to determine policies involving the enrollment and assignment of pupils and a plan for annual promotions
19. Make reports to the church, the Board of Christian Education, and parents
20. Seek to establish friendly relationships with the homes of the church and help arrange parent-teacher meetings
21. Work in close cooperation with the pastor and DCE
22. Keep up with new trends and ideas by reading books and magazines on Christian Education and attending conferences and conventions
23. Help nominate department superintendents, teachers and other workers
24. Assist in making decisions concerning curricular materials and supplies
25. Help set up rules and regulations concerning the operation of the school
26. Supervise the keeping of records and utilize them for school improvement
27. Help to set up an absentee follow-up system

28. Stress the importance of evangelism and missions in all groups
29. Constantly study the use of space and the grading system
30. Give particular attention to the curricular elements of music, memory work, and media education
31. See that the Sunday School opens and closes on time

As a Supervisor

1. Oversee the work of teachers and classes
2. Constantly stress the need for quality and improvement
3. Assist in the evaluation and measurement of progress and achievement
4. Stress the need for accomplishment
5. Help set up objectives for the total program in general and for teaching and learning in particular – both spiritual and academic
6. Call for objectives for children, youth and adult work
7. Help make available materials and tools for teaching and working
8. Stress the importance of good morale and good working conditions
9. Make himself/herself available to all workers for personal counseling
10. Provide assistance in solving problems in teaching and learning
11. Work with the pastor, the DCE, and the Board in setting up and operating a program of leadership education and development
12. Constantly study how to create a good environment for workers to improve themselves, work together, and get results

Pre-session Duties

1. Be present at least 30 minutes early to make preparation for the day
2. Use this time occasionally for prayer, getting acquainted, and checking on staff and equipment

Session and Sunday Duties

1. Where used, open the general assembly session for worship
2. Help to greet people
3. Stress the importance of planning ahead in worship services
4. Make any announcements necessary
5. Direct the classes to their rooms
6. See that literature is distributed
7. Check on the presence of teachers and workers
8. Watch particularly the work of the General Secretary and Registrar
9. Urge all officers, teachers, workers and pupils to attend the church services
10. Urge all workers to attend the business and training sessions provided for them
11. Where used, conduct the closing session; do not run into the time for the preaching service
12. Be on the alert for needs and achievements of the classes and departments

Weekday Duties

1. Keep the Sunday School properly organized by maintaining it intact; by stressing enlargement, by enlisting proper officers, and by seeing that the classes are functioning
2. Direct promotional activities through regular visitation and advertising
3. Keep the records intact
4. Maintain meetings and standards
5. Train officers, teachers and workers
6. Lead in evangelistic activities
7. Plan for social life and fellowship activities
8. Plan ahead for the coming Sunday; try some experiments occasionally
9. Express appreciation for the work of officers, teachers and pupils
10. Examine last Sunday's reports and records
11. Contact the ill and absent workers and pupils

Monthly Duties

1. Attend the meetings of the Board of Christian Education
2. Urge all workers to also attend this meeting
3. See that the annual program calendar is worked month-by-month
4. Where used, meet with department superintendents in their meetings
5. Conduct the work of the Committee on Administration (officers)
6. Check on rooms and equipment with the teachers
7. Check to see that the standards are being upheld
8. Preside at Workers' conferences
9. Watch attendance trends

Annual Duties

1. Provide for an annual census, probably in September
2. See that equipment is adequate for another year
3. Determine what improvements are needed
4. Plan to attend Sunday School conferences and conventions
5. Help plan a year's program (work with pastor, DCE, and Board)
6. Help set up the financial program in the light of the annual plans
7. Assist with plans for the annual vacation Bible school
8. Make reports to the church and denomination
9. Send an annual letter of themes to all workers
10. Help plan an annual worker's banquet
11. Revise standards

General Duties

1. Be courteous
2. Welcome visitors and new pupils
3. Be enthusiastic always
4. Tell of the success of the Sunday School
5. Compliment worthy deeds and activities of individuals, departments and classes
6. Read books on Sunday School work – at least one per year
7. Remember – you are pastor of the Sunday School
8. Meditate on the school – compare, analyze, and evaluate

Outside Duties

1. Publicize the work of Christian Education
2. Talk it up
3. Invite people
4. Inform people
5. Tell pastor and teachers of prospects
6. Represent the church and church school in public affairs
7. Be cooperative with other churches and good causes in the community
8. Keep a memo book for suggestions, records and appointments

Duties of Associate Superintendents*

*The number of these superintendents in each church will vary according to the needs of the church and school, the type and shape of the buildings and equipment, the number of workers to be administered, and the degree of emphasis placed by the church on such matters as evangelism, visitation, enlargement, etc.

Associate General Superintendent
1. Preside in the absence of the General Superintendent
2. Help the General Superintendent each Sunday and through the week
3. Assume special assignments such as curriculum, membership, training

Superintendent of Enlargement
1. Be responsible for increasing enrollment
2. Check upon progress made
3. Seek to discover prospects
4. Assign prospects to workers
5. Invite prospects intelligently
6. Welcome new members
7. Study causes of absences
8. Follow up every absence
9. Direct visitation and all enlistment efforts

Superintendent of Evangelism
1. Work with pastor, DCE, and Superintendent in making and/or keeping all efforts positively evangelistic
2. Work with all enlargement
3. Make available resources on personal witnessing
4. Provide training opportunities in evangelistic visitation
5. Provide guidance for participation by all workers in each revival effort
6. Cooperate with all denominational plans for evangelism

Superintendent of Training
1. Serve on the Committee of Leadership Training
2. Study the training needs of the school and the church
3. Check on the training records of all workers
4. Propose training opportunities
5. Recommend individual study of books
6. Lead in providing specialized training
7. Order materials for training program
8. Plan a training program for prospects
9. Work with all agencies in the church to study and plan training
10. Serve as resource person in ideas, counseling and materials
11. Develop a Christian philosophy of training and service for the church
12. Call attention to the program of of study recommended by the denomination

Other Possibilities
1. Superintendent of Social Life
2. Superintendent of Attendance
3. Superintendent of Education
4. Superintendent of Missions
5. Divisional Superintendents
6. Superintendent of Equipment
7. Superintendent of Publicity, etc.

Duties of the Church School Secretary

As a Recorder

1. Keep the minutes of all Sunday School meetings
2. Prepare a docket from these minutes for the Chairman of the Board of Christian Education
3. Keep a record of finances
4. Be responsible for the record system

As a Correspondent

1. Write all letters where necessary
2. If not otherwise designated, order Sunday School literature

As a Statistician

1. Reserve and report statistics of each session of the Sunday School
2. Get reports from department and class secretaries; such reports will cover constituency, enrollment, attendance, offerings, and achievements
3. Make information readily available to all official workers; report trends

Sunday Duties

1. Instruct department and class secretaries on records
2. Cooperate with all officers and workers in making information available
3. Do not interrupt classes to distribute and collect record books
4. Be on time; if absent, get someone to serve in your place
5. Have on hand forms, literature, and records at all times
6. If have a Registrar, take your place near him and cooperate
7. See that class record books are in the hands of the class secretaries
8. Collect class reports
9. Make a report for the Sunday School
10. Where used, make a report at the closing assembly period (not much used anymore)

Monthly Duties

1. Attend Board of Christian Education meeting; be ready to make a report
2. Prepare a statistical report for the Board when called for
3. If secretary of the Board, keep the minutes
4. Attend any other meetings which will provide assistance in your work and in which you can help

General Duties

1. Prepare reports for church conferences
2. Order literature for people
3. Prepare statistical reports for the General Superintendent
4. Be neat, quick, and accurate; stress good records; talk up the Sunday School
5. Help foster stewardship education; attend church services
6. Avoid consistent absences

Duties of the Church School Treasurer

1. Receive the church school offering each week from the church school secretary
2. Enter the totals of this offering into the check book of the church school
3. Deposit this offering each week in the bank
4. Post the disbursements and receipts in the ledger at the time of their occurrence
5. Give a monthly report of receipts and expenditures when called for
6. Write out and send checks for church school bills
7. Make out an annual report for the church year
8. See that the books are audited annually
9. Be an officer of the church school; be responsible to both the church school as a whole and to the congregation as a whole; therefore, be prepared at any time to give an account of the finances of the church school
10. Serve as chairman of the finance committee of the church school
11. With the help of the pastor, general superintendent, and a committee on finance, prepare an annual budget
12. Make a report of benevolence giving, stressing the cause of missionary giving
13. By various means, inform the Sunday School constituency of the Scriptural principles involved in giving
14. Distribute literature on stewardship; make and display posters that stimulate giving; mail letters about the importance of Sunday School giving
15. Inspire the teachers to make "offering time" a time of genuine worship

Duties of Church Administrator or Business Manager

1. Review the complete past financial program of the church; study total needs now
2. Work with committee on finance to compile a church budget
3. Work with them in developing ways and means of meeting the budget
4. Report to the official Board on the financial status of the church

Duties of the Registrar*
*Office used mostly in the larger churches

As a Recorder

1. Keep classification records of individual pupils
2. Keep enrollment cards to show name, address, birthday, church affiliation, etc., of each pupil ; keep this up to date
3. Keep record of the department, class and teacher of each pupil regarding attendance, visitation, growth, and permanent records of achievements

As a Correspondent

1. Prepare a monthly report on each pupil for parents
2. Follow up absentees and reports to pupils, teachers and parents

As a Statistician

1. Keep records of the weekly standing of each pupil; this includes his attendance, punctuality, offerings given, study of lesson, church attendance, and use of the Bible (used with 4-6 Point Record System)
2. Average the monthly grades of each pupil; sends out report cards to homes
3. Issue promotion certificates and awards

Sunday Duties

1. Be on time; if absent, provide a substitute
2. Have on hand forms, literature, and records at all times
3. Cooperate with the general secretary at all times
4. Assist the secretary in seeing that class books are available to class secretaries
5. Make out permanent records on all new pupils; see that they get to classes
6. Be ready to assist with records
7. Help with the absentee follow-up system

Monthly Duties

1. Record monthly grades of each pupil in the record system
2. Prepare report cards for each pupil; note honor roll achievers
3. Attend all business meetings

General Duties

1. Help make plans for Promotion and/or Rally Day
2. Have certificates, seals, diplomas, etc., ready for those days
3. Record such information on the permanent record cards for each pupil
4. Cooperate in all extension efforts, assign and classify all prospects and new pupils
5. Be informed thoroughly about the curriculum and grading system
6. Cooperate with all departmental workers; be neat, quick, and accurate
7. Promote the school, be enthusiastic; attend all church services

Duties of the Literature Secretary*
*Used where the General Sunday School Secretary does not order literature

1. Urge secretaries, Superintendents, and others to order supplies and literature well in advance
2. Distribute literature and supplies
3. Direct processing of class reports
4. Keep an adequate supply of non-durable general supplies
5. Dispose of outdated materials
6. Attend monthly meetings of the church school for business and training
7. Solicit quarterly curriculum material requests from each class, and checks that the requests are reasonable in terms of type of material and quantity
8. Order special study material when requested and authorized by the superintendent and/or ministers

Duties of the Secretary of Technology

1. Maintain a catalog of equipment
2. Keep the equipment in good operating condition, particularly the computers
3. Schedule the use of equipment; study new developments and the whole field
4. Furnish trained operators when required
5. Have the equipment set up where and when requested
6. Maintain the library of records, filmstrips, films, videos, CD's and DVD's and check them in and out as required; make provisions for previewing materials
7. Order equipment when requested and approved by the Board of Education
8. Attend Sunday School regularly and make arrangements for a capable substitute

Duties of the Church Librarian

1. Plan with the pastor and proper committee of the Board of Christian Education in all matters of general policy regarding the library facilities and services
2. Consult frequently with leaders as to their needs in literature and pictures
3. Advise the proper committee concerning needs, and recommend materials for purchase
4. Submit budget requirements for library materials at stated intervals
5. Inform church leaders and members of available library resources
6. Set up library procedures: catalog, books, publications, pictures, and classification
7. Label and prepare books, publications, and pictures for circulation
8. See that proper record is made of all resources loaned
9. Keep record of the types of persons using the library for guidance in selecting new materials
10. Keep church members informed about the library; stimulate interest by special book displays, exhibits, story hours, book reviews, etc.
11. Supply the local newspaper with interesting stories or information regarding library resources, particularly in connection with specific developments within the community

Duties of the Committee on Church School Administration*

*The duties of this committee are placed here because its nature involves the work of the General Church School Superintendent together with that of the other general officers under his supervision; also known as Sunday School Council or Sunday School Cabinet.

Composition

With the General Superintendent as chairman, the membership is composed of the pastor, the DCE, and all general officers, including the secretary and treasurer.

Purpose

The committee facilitates the work of the general officers and conducts the business of the church school.

Duties

1. Check on the plans and policies of the Board of Christian Education and translate such matters into the work of the school
2. Constantly review the work of the church school
3. Check on the needs of the various departments and units of the school
4. Take care of routine business matters
5. Hear reports of the work and assist the General Superintendent in the general administration of the church school
6. Help make plans for the departments and classes
7. Provide assistance in program and calendar planning
8. Make regular checks on the financial status of the church school
9. Consider solutions to any problems which may arise
10. Assist the various general officers in the planning and execution of their responsibilities
11. Serve as a clearing house for all problems and directives
12. Periodically check on the progress achieved
13. Make sure that the functions of administration, organization and supervision are adequately accomplished
14. Meet monthly with procedures controlled by usual parliamentary methods
15. Call for meetings at the divisional and departmental levels, and call for reports of the work of these groups

Duties of the Worship Chairman of the Children's Department

1. Be responsible to plan and execute a fifteen minute worship service for the Junior Department
2. Occasionally permit Juniors to worship in the church sanctuary
3. Set aside a time in each session for learning new hymns and songs
4. Allow juniors to arrange their own worship centers
5. Attempt to bring the children to a feeling of God's presence and consciousness of a relationship with Him
6. Remember that the atmosphere of a place of worship is essential
7. Make sure that the temperature of the room is comfortable
8. See that each person is quiet and attentive
9. Be well-prepared
10. Choose materials with the needs and interests of the children in mind

SECTION FOUR

WORKERS IN THE SUNDAY CHURCH SCHOOL

Common Responsibilities and Duties of Superintendents

In many churches one will find both divisional and departmental superintendents. Certain types of duties and responsibilities are common to both, such as the following:

1. Be thoroughly familiar with the objectives and the denominational materials for the age groups concerned
2. Be sure that the division or department is properly graded and that recommended materials are used
3. Be regular in attendance; arrive early to make sure all is in readiness and to deal with possible emergencies or adjustments
4. Make sure that the departments open and close promptly, remembering that the session begins when the first pupil arrives
5. Report regularly to the governing body of the church school regarding progress, needs, and special problems
6. Take advantage as much as possible of all training opportunities
7. Give adequate notice to the division or general superintendent if necessary to be absent or to resign

General Duties of the Division Superintendents

1. Give assistance to the General Superintendent, sometimes organizing an executive council of the church school
2. Act as chairman of the divisional council of workers, including departmental superintendents of the Sunday School and other workers in the division
3. See that an adequate staff of workers is maintained in the division
4. See that divisional workers are trained
5. See that the best possible provision is made for space, equipment, and materials for the division
6. Confer with divisional workers
7. Observe the best principles or organization in the division
8. Plan for inter-departmental activities
9. Promote inter-departmental social life and fellowship
10. Constantly search for prospective workers
11. Seek greater understanding of the principle of grading in the division
12. Plan the recommendations and reports to the Board of Christian Education
13. Consider ways of executing Board policies in the division
14. Represent the division in church education in meetings of all kinds
15. Specialize in supervision; seek self-improvement; keep accurate records
16. Cooperate fully with other general officers
17. Guide new department superintendents in understanding the work of their group
18. Supervise the work of all departments in the division
19. Maintain a list of persons willing to serve as substitute teachers
20. Encourage evangelistic outreach by the classes
21. Study financial needs and prepare budgetary requests when required
22. Relate all the work of the division to the total program of the church

Duties of the Superintendents of the Children's Departments and Regulations
(consult these ahead)

Study common duties of superintendents listed previously.

1. Acknowledge the leading of the Holy Spirit in accepting your duties
2. Be responsible for the spiritual oversight of your departments through prayer and devotion to your calling as superintendent
3. Be responsible for the recruiting and training of teachers for your division
4. Arrange for supply teachers in case of the absence of your regular teachers
5. Meet with your teachers each month for the purpose of discussing needs, problems, and recommendations in regard to your division
6. Represent your division at Board of Christian Education meetings
7. Carry out the plans for the division in the Board meeting
8. Attend, as much as possible, the training sessions during the church year
9. Be responsible for the maintenance of supplies for your division which includes keeping a close watch on department literature to see that it is ordered and delivered on time
10. Be responsible for keeping close supervision on the rooms of your division, seeing that they are in order and are adequately supplied for the sessions
11. See that all of your teachers are on time
12. Keep, as a matter of personal and departmental assistance, personal records on the running of your division; this should include a record of attendance, program, and plans and ideas for the future
13. Strive to maintain more personal contact with pupils, in order to obtain better attendance and deeper worship attitudes, and create better discipline
14. Attempt to obtain better parent-teacher conferences as a means of promoting the evangelistic emphasis of the division
15. Set goals annually and report them to the Board
16. See that pupils are properly graded
17. Help select workers for your division
18. Keep spiritual and academic objectives before all workers
19. Secure department standards and use them to operate
20. Work with the General Superintendent in planning workers' conferences each month
21. Report Board policies to the division and study means of implementing them
22. Study the needs and concerns of children in the church and community
23. Serve as liaison with organizations, persons, and resources in and beyond the local church which relate to children
24. Supervise Nursery, Kindergarten, and Vacation Bible Schools and all special day programs

Children's Division Regulations (A Sample)
Sunday School Staff
General Information: to all Teachers and Workers

"Therefore, my beloved brethren, be ye steadfast, unmovable, always abounding in the work of the Lord, for as much as ye know that your labor is not in vain in the Lord."(I Cor 15:58)

I. YOUR TEACHING MINISTRY
   God called you to this high and noble task. "And He Himself appointed some to be,,,,,teachers, in order to fully equip His people for the work of serving....for the building of Christ's body." (Eph 4:11)

   A. Your teaching is of eternal significance; the result will last forever.
   B. Teaching is more than just imparting facts. It involves presenting Bible truths in such a way that lives and attitudes are changed.
   C. Pray that God will make you a channel of His love. Remember each of of your students, one by one, in your daily prayer.
   D. Evangelism's chief field is the Sunday School. Our work is not to rebuild human ruins but to build lives into Christ from their earliest years. Our aim is to bring the scholar at the earliest moment into a conscious and intimate relationship to God as Father, to Christ as Savior and Friend, and to the Spirit of Truth.
   E. Present the claims of Jesus Christ to your students periodically and give them the opportunity to make the decision to follow Him.

II. TIMING

   A. If Sunday School begin at 9:30, please be present at least 15 minutes before that time. Your class begins with the arrival of the first child. Roll books will be in your room.
   B. Remember that Junior Department worship service is from 9:30 to 9:50. Sit with your class and participate during worship time. Do not let a child in your group disturb others.
   C. Give teachers time to conclude the lesson and hand out papers—first closing bell will ring at 10:25. Do not dismiss at this time. Second bell for dismissal is at 10:30.
   D. Please let the superintendent know early in the week if you cannot be present the following Sunday. If at all possible, have your own preferred substitute; discuss the needs of your class with him and give him your teacher's manual.

III. KEEPING OF RECORDS

   A. Our Sunday School secretary has requested that all teachers fill out the the information on the front of the offering envelopes. (Church school report)
   B. Attendance records must be accurate if award system is to be effective and meaningful.
      1. Only excused absences are for illness or attendance at another Sunday School.
      2. Mark an X or ex for an excused absence.

3. Be sure to ask a regularly attending child about his absence the next Sunday. He may forget to tell you.
4. Registration forms are available for new students.

C. Absentees
1. Please set a system within your class to check on pupils whose attendance is irregular. Have one or more of his friends within the class contact him to let him know that he was missed; then report the reason for his absence to the teacher. If a pupil is absent two or more consecutive Sundays, the teacher, as well as the other children, should contact him or the parents.
2. At the end of each month, please give the superintendent a list of those absent without a valid reason for two or more Sundays consecutively. The superintendent can visit the home and talk to the parents and the child about the importance of regular attendance at Sunday School. The teacher and the other pupils should pray for the absentees. This is an effort to prevent children from dropping out of our Sunday School, and let them know they are loved and missed when they are not in class.
3. Please use absentee cards which are available in the cabinet.

IV. LITERATURE AND SUPPLIES

A. At the first of each quarter, be prepared to turn in all unused materials from the preceding quarter – to be filed for use the next year.
B. Keep partially used books; they can be used for visitors. Don't give out a book until the child has been present two Sundays. Be sure each child's name is on his book.
C. Inform the superintendent of any additional materials you feel would be helpful. We want to provide teachers with all the materials and aids they need, but, as stewards of the Lord's funds, we should avoid any unnecessary expenditures.
D. Keep these supplies available in the general cabinet: staples, scotch tape, stars, pencils, chalk, white paper, paste, scissors, felt marking pens, clips, fasteners, and some pictures. Please return materials to cabinet at the close of lesson or when finished with.

V. OFFERINGS

A. Emphasize the need of giving cheerfully and systematically to the Lord's work.
B. Don't let the offering become just an incidental thing. Stress the truth: "The Lord loves a 'cheerful' giver." Teach them to "sacrifice" some study time, chewing gum, candy, etc. during the week to bring an offering to the Lord.
C. Bring a graph or chart to show a quarter's offering record.

VI. YOUR ROOM

A. Try to make your room as attractive and interesting as possible.
B. Keep shelves and cupboards orderly. At the end of the class period, with assigned student help, straighten the room and set it in order.

C. Inform the superintendent of anything your room needs, or needs to have done—tables, chairs, coat hooks, bulletin boards, chalk boards, etc.
D. Provide some kind of waste paper basket.

Duties of the Superintendent of the Youth Division

1. Be thoroughly familiar with the objectives and the denominational materials for the age group; study the needs and concerns of youth.
2. Be sure the group is properly graded and the recommended materials are used.
3. Be regular in attendance and arrive early.
4. Be sure the group opens and closes promptly.
5. Report regularly to the governing body.
6. Take advantage of training opportunities.
7. Give general assistance to the General Superintendent.
8. See that an adequate staff of workers is maintained.
9. See that department workers are trained.
10. See that the best possible provision is made for space, equipment, and materials.
11. Observe the best principles of organization in the departments.
12. Plan for inter-departmental activities.
13. Promote inter-departmental social life and fellowship.
14. Specialize in supervision.
15. Constantly seek self-improvement.
16. Represent the departments in Board meetings.
17. See that each department develops enrollment procedures.
18. Conduct divisional and department meetings each month.
19. Set goals annually and report them to the Board of Education.
20. Keep spiritual and academic objectives uppermost.
21. Work with the General Superintendent in planning a workers' conference each month.
22. Report Board policies to the division and study means of implementing them.
23. Coordinate the program plans of all youth activities in order to have a unified and comprehensive ministry with youth; create a youth calendar.
24. Serve as liaison with organizations, persons and resources in and beyond the local church which relate to youth.
25. Bring together the appropriate workers and parents with problems.
26. Where a youth minister is present on the staff, cooperate with him.
27. Where present, serve as chairman of the divisional Council, calling regular meetings to review the present status of the work and to develop new plans.

Duties of the Superintendent of the Adult Division

1. Be able to lead and follow.
2. Maintain a strong Christian character, a clean, moral life, and deep faith.
3. Feel a divine call to your work.
4. Be a Bible student.
5. Give liberally.
6. Have compassion for the lost.
7. Gain specific training in educational psychology.
8. Gain the proficiency of a specialist in the curriculum materials of your division.
9. Act as chairman of business meetings and monthly departmental conferences, working closely with General Superintendent.
10. Be responsible for the organization of your division.
11. See that your division is Christ-centered, Bible-based, pupil-related, and properly graded.
12. Set goals for the entire year, and report to the Board of Education.
13. Study the work of the division, and build a comprehensive, well-balanced program.
14. Guide your teachers in formulating and adopting a teacher's covenant.
15. See that adequate space is provided for each class.
16. Keep spiritual and academic objectives before your division.
17. Secure department standards and compare them with your division.
18. Grade and group adults.
19. Be in charge of worship. (when used)
20. Work with the Pastor and General Superintendent in seeing that soul winning at home and abroad is emphasized, studied, and practiced in the departments.
21. Secure and increase enrollments to increase attendance.
22. Ensure the keeping of good records.
23. See that all departmental activities are coordinated into an efficiently functional unit.
24. Work with the General Superintendent in planning workers' conferences.
25. Report Board policies to the division and study means of implementing them.
26. Make plans to operate an adequate Home Department.
27. Recommend classes and study groups for adults.
28. Study the needs of adults and help to set goals for the work.
29. Serve as liaison with organizations, persons, and resources in and beyond the local church which relate to adults.
30. Represent adults in meetings of church groups.

Duties of Department Superintendents

Preparation Duties

1. Study the work of the department
2. Conduct personal, inward preparation
    a. Get hold of God in faith and fellowship
    b. Be willing to work and sacrifice to do the job
    c. Get a vision of the work to be done and the possibilities for growth
    d. Cultivate a good personality and a pleasing disposition
    e. Walk with God
3. Conduct personal, mechanical preparation
    a. Know the organizational machinery of the work
    b. Keep abreast of books, study courses, and free literature
    c. Know the prospects of the department
    d. Learn to advise every worker in the department
4. Conduct personal preparation to meet individual needs
    a. Of the careless, indifferent, and discouraged worker
    b. Of the dissatisfied worker
    c. In times of death, sickness, sorrow, etc.

General Duties

1. Attend workers' conferences with all workers
2. Be a pastor to your department
3. Direct the attraction and retention of attendees
4. Attend all church services

As an Organizer

1. See that the department is properly grouped and graded
2. See that you have an adequate staff of teachers
3. See that you have adequate staff of workers and teachers
4. Be sure you have an adequate teaching staff on Sundays

As an Administrator

1. Cooperate with the divisional superintendent in the total program
2. Plan a well-balanced program in the department
3. Cooperate with all other department superintendents
4. See that the record system operates properly
5. Study the curriculum materials
6. Constantly stress visitation and evangelism
7. Adopt an absentee follow-up system
8. See that you have proper facilities and equipment
9. Promote the interests and activities of the department
10. Prepare worship programs (where used)
11. See that the department secretary does the job properly
12. Maintain a group of informed associate and substitute teachers who are familiar with the teaching program and materials, and be able to assist on call

13. Give requisitions for supplies and literature to the general secretary
14. Distribute new materials to teachers: each unit, month or quarter
15. See that usable supplies are returned and filed after a unit is completed
16. Arrange in advance for special needs, such as media supplies
17. Schedule and preside at department meetings, each month or before each new unit of study (see agenda below); preside, ordinarily, at all general sessions of the department
18. Encourage church membership for all pupils of proper age
19. Plan ways to contact and cooperate with the parents; i.e. parent-teacher meetings, visitation in homes at least once a year, parents' visits to the Sunday morning sessions of the department, use of "parent sponsors" to help with visitation and the social affairs of the group
20. Notify teachers if absence is necessary, asking one of them to act as substitute

As a Supervisor

1. See that all workers in the department are trained
2. Work constantly for the improvement of teaching
3. Keep spiritual and academic objectives uppermost
4. Develop a department standard
5. Learn how to get people to do things and enjoy it
6. Watch the class work
7. Be alert to meet individual needs of teachers and pupils
8. Direct expressional activities
9. Maintain regular conferences with workers
10. Be constantly alert to the needs and growth of the pupils; strive to evaluate the teaching program by its apparent effect on the beliefs, character, and daily lives of the participants
11. Promote improved teaching methods and heightened morale; be sure each teacher has a sense of satisfaction through striving to do increasingly effective work; provide personal help between department meetings for each unit in progress
12. Plan with the teachers for opportunities of spiritual and professional growth, such as workers' conferences, leadership courses, use of the church school library, observation in corresponding class of other well-managed church school or public school, summer conferences, laboratory classes, correspondence courses, etc.

Sunday Duties
1. Be present early; at least 15 minutes in advance
2. Conduct any worship services in the department
3. Check about teachers, officers, and workers for the department
4. Be ready to teach or help where needed
5. Visit and study the needs of the classes
6. Instruct the class secretaries and department secretary
7. Know how to use the class record book; see that reports are made to the general secretary
8. See that information about new pupils is reported
9. Check on literature and absentees; help distribute literature
10. Provide for vacancies of teachers

Monthly Duties

1. Attend all business meetings without fail
2. Prepare for department meetings each month
3. See that all workers and teachers attend the monthly meetings
4. Call on absentees and sick in the department
5. Assign others to visit; sponsor a visitation day

Annual Duties

1. Supervise the curriculum of the department in collaboration with the teachers; do not dictate in this matter to the teachers
2. See that teacher training is carried out in your department
3. See that pupils are graded and promoted
4. Consult the General Superintendent about facilities, equipment and supplies
5. Encourage the Pastor to instruct the teachers in evangelism
6. Make plans to take care of new pupils in a canvas

How to Conduct Department Meetings Each Month

1. Open meeting with prayer
2. Have the secretary call the roll and read the minutes
3. Discuss class matters and problems, class by class
4. Report all sick and absentee pupils
5. Report visits in the interest of pupils
6. Discuss procedures for new pupils
7. Evaluate the facilities, equipment and supplies
8. Discuss the condition of the rooms
9. Determine discipline policies
10. Evaluate the record keeping system
11. Determine whether everyone knows their job
12. Plan for teacher training and evangelism
13. Plan worship services and special programs
14. Explore methods of teaching
15. Discuss the lessons for the month and how to use and teach them
16. Plan recreational events
17. Establish procedures for visitation
18. Creatively plan Christmas and Easter programs
19. Discuss individual problems and interests

Duties of General Department Workers

Associate Superintendent

1. Give general assistance to the Department Superintendent
2. Be prepared to teach in the department
3. Be willing to help in other groups outside the Sunday School, such as VBS
4. Serve as counselor
5. Be present 10 or 15 minutes early on Sundays
6. Be responsible for the signal system in the department
7. Lead workers in visitation
8. Protect the department from interruptions
9. Assist late comers and visitors
10. Be responsible for department growth
11. Be responsible for absentees
12. Promote teacher training
13. Promote home cooperation
14. Study and know pupils
15. Attend workers' meetings
16. Serve as librarian
17. Check on workers' attendance at department meetings
18. Help arrange the assembly room
19. Train vice presidents of organized classes

Department Secretary

1. Be responsible for department records; be punctual; arrive early
2. Make out reports which require record information
3. Check attendance in Nursery and Beginner Departments
4. Submit needs for supplies and materials to the General Secretary and others
5. May be responsible for the signal for the department
6. Train workers in the use of records, particularly class secretaries
7. Secure and keep department enrollment; keep up-to-date prospect list and absentees
8. Supply information for workers and teachers at department meetings
9. Classify pupils; record birthdays; keep records on all pupil achievements
10. Mark records of all children in the Beginner Department
11. Teach all department officers how to use the record system
12. Keep department minutes

Pianist

1. Be present 10 to 15 minutes in advance of the opening bell
2. Play softly during pre-session periods
3. Plan special things for the pre-session period at times
4. Gear music to the theme of the lesson of the day
5. Play very simply in the Children's Division
6. Serve as an associate teacher during the class period.
7. Assist the other workers during the class period
8. Promote stewardship and missions in the department
9. Play appropriately for different occasions
10. Memorize frequently-used songs and choruses

Chorister

1. Help plan music for the opening worship period; at other times
2. Lead singing wherever needed
3. Do not show off
4. Assist other workers during the class period
5. Serve as an associate teacher
6. Collect music from all sources useful for the department
7. Keep departmental instruments in tune
8. Help classes learn new music
9. Train pupils in musical skills
10. Maintain a cheerful spirit in the department
11. May be responsible for fellowship and service activities
12. Greet pupils and newcomers

Librarian

1. See that study materials and story papers go to classes
2. Place all materials before the class period begins
3. Be custodian of materials and equipment for the department
4. Store all excess materials and supplies
5. File pictures and materials for the department
6. File all media materials and equipment
7. Check out any projection equipment from the church library
8. Promote good reading
9. Study reading needs, habits, and interests of the pupils

Associates

1. Serve as general helpers wherever needed in the department
2. Be subject to officers and teachers

Associate (Substitute) Teachers

1. Have lesson materials at hand
2. Attend workers' meetings
3. Study the work of teaching and be available for teaching at all times
4. Cooperate with regular teachers; visit classes and take part

General Patterns of Responsibility*
*Some department superintendents may find it helpful to use the following general pattern of responsibility for department workers.

WORKER	PRIMARY RESPONSIBILITY	SECONDARY DUTIES
Department Superintendent	Evangelism, administration and supervision	Train class presidents
Associate Superintendent	Aid in growth, training, follow-up	Train class vice pres.
Department Secretary	Keep records, supplies, materials	Train class secretaries
Pianist	Accompany music	Stress Stewardship
Chorister	Singing, music training	Promote missions, fellowship and service
Librarian	Act as Department librarian	Promote reading
Teachers	Conduct instruction, evangelism	Foster home-church relations

THE CRADLE ROLL DEPARTMENT

Duties of the Cradle Roll Superintendent
(See Department Superintendent)

As an Administrator

1. Be sure that the Cradle Roll Department is properly organized for work in the home and at the church
2. Maintain an overall view of the department as it functions in the home and in the church
3. Guide and inspire the workers, and look for additional personnel with varied abilities that your department requires
4. Conduct the business meetings of the department (See agenda for departmental superintendent)
5. Conduct monthly meetings of training for workers in evangelism and visitation
6. Share progress and achievements with the workers and others
7. Represent the department in all church and Sunday meetings where required; give reports and seek financial support for your group
8. Be constantly on the alert for good ideas, resources, and materials
9. Attend conferences and conventions
10. Publicize the work of the department; keep the work of the department before the church and the community; be on the lookout for prospects
11. Plan for an annual Cradle Roll Day
12. Plan monthly meetings with mothers for study and inspiration
13. Plan an annual party for parents

As an Instructor
1. Assist in enlisting a sufficient number of capable teachers of expectant parents and parents of children three years of age and under who are not attending Sunday School
2. Order and distribute the literature and supplies needed for teaching
3. See that space and equipment for teaching improvement are provided

4. Interpret to the workers the teaching assignment of the department
5. Provide training opportunities for the workers
6. Provide Christian literature which will help Christian parents

As an Evangelist

1. Analyze the church territory, dividing it into small areas for locating and visiting prospects and enrolling babies
2. Interpret what it means to reach a person
3. Interpret the techniques of effective visitation
4. Involve other Sunday School workers in reaching Cradle Role family members
5. Win unsaved parents to Christ

As a Church Worker

1. Guide all workers in the department to do the work of the church
2. Study the records to ascertain the progress being made
3. Help workers and parents to be loyal supporters of the local church

Duties of Workers in the Cradle Roll Department

Associate Superintendent

1. Provide general assistance to the Superintendent
2. Assist in visiting prospects and members
3. Participate in all training opportunities
4. Lead in locating expectant parents and prospects
5. Keep standards high

Cradle Roll Secretary

1. Keep accurate and up-to-date records of all babies enrolled
2. Keep good records on all workers, their responsibilities and assignments
3. Supply lists of needed literature and supplies to the General Secretary
4. See that Christian literature for parents and others is available
5. Be prepared to submit periodic reports on the work to the Superintendent
6. Help visitors to observe the birthdays of the children
7. Watch the newspapers for the birth of new babies

Cradle Roll Visitation Worker

1. Pray much about your work in the homes of the babies
2. Participate in training opportunities provided
3. Take Bible study materials and other Christian literature into the home
4. Be constantly on the lookout for new prospects
5. Prepare regular reports on the work of visitation in the home
6. Provide assistance to parents on worship, witnessing and Bible study

7. Minister to any personal needs you may find in your visits
8. Invite parents to attend the Cradle Roll Department classes and socials
9. Welcome parents who come to church and Sunday School; be helpful

THE NURSERY DEPARTMENT

Duties of the Nursery Department Superintendent
(See Department Superintendent)

1. Be a dedicated Christian who is concerned with the telling of the story of Christ to pre-school children
2. See that the Nursery is adequately supplied with supplies and toys for the children; a room needs from 25-35 square feet per pupil
3. Create close relations with the children's parents and attempt to solicit their help in the upkeep and supervision of the Nursery
4. Work closely with the General Superintendent in matters concerning the Nursery Department
5. Prepare lessons diligently and thoroughly so that the children may get the most possible benefit of them
6. Attend all meetings where the department is involved as a representative of the department
7. Strive to keep up to date as to the best methods for teaching in the department, availing self of every training opportunity
8. Give a good testimony to the children in attitude, conduct and word
9. Take an interest in the needs and desires of children and take an interest in their salvation, keeping this always in mind as the prime goal of teaching and working
10. Coordinate teaching emphasis with the goals and aims of both the department and those of the church school as a whole
11. In accordance with the policy of the church, help discover and enlist enough associates and helpers to keep the ratio of one worker for every 6-8 pupils enrolled in the department
12. Visit all the homes at least once a year
13. Assign each worker a group of children (members and prospects) to connect regularly and to visit at least once a quarter, and help them learn more about children and better ways of teaching
14. Plan and conduct the department officers' and teachers' meetings
15. Be responsible for the Sunday morning procedures; take charge of group activities or delegate them to other workers
16. Be in the room about 30 minutes early and greet early comers
17. See that the extended sessions, if used, are well planned and well staffed; take turns with other department workers in staffing the extended sessions
18. Promote parent-worker meetings

Duties of Workers in the Nursery Department

<u>Associate Superintendent</u>

1. Share responsibilities with the Superintendent
2. Visit regularly, at least once a quarter, the home assigned

3. Communicate with each enrolled child (assigned for visitation) when he is absent or when he has special needs
4. Deliver literature, before the first day of each quarter, to homes (members and prospects) assigned
5. Participate In officers' and teachers' meetings and other training opportunities
6. Share in the responsibility of repairing, cleaning and arranging materials that are placed in the room
7. Be in the room before the children arrive
8. Take turns with other department workers in staffing the morning extended sessions (when used)
9. Keep the standards high for the department

Nursery Secretary

See the duties listed under the work of the Secretary in the Cradle Department

Nursery Associates and Assistants

1. Arrive early to prepare for the work of the day and greet early comers
2. Help with children as they arrive
3. Welcome parents and help them in any way possible
4. Help with the home contacts, visit, and take materials to the home
5. Help conduct the program for the day at Sunday School

THE BEGINNER DEPARTMENT

Duties of the Beginner Department Superintendent
(See Department Superintendent)

1. Be a good example of a follower of Jesus Christ so that children will learn of Him by watching you
2. Pray for the children and all workers in your department
3. Make thorough preparation for teaching If you serve as a lead teacher
4. Coordinate the work of several teachers or rooms of children where needed
5. Be responsible for the program of the department as a whole
6. Hold teachers' and workers' meetings to plan ahead
7. See that all materials are ordered in advance
8. Organize and assign responsibilities for Sunday morning
9. Plan the visitation program for the department
10. Cooperate with all other departments
11. Inspire workers in your department with a vision of the importance of the work
12. Supervise the teaching processes

Duties of Workers in the Beginner Department

Beginner Department Secretary

1. Keep all the records of the department
2. Take roll and offering each Sunday without disturbing children and workers
3. See duties of the Department Secretary for more general duties
4. Be ready to help other workers

Beginner Department Pianist

1. Remember that you are a teacher, too
2. Be prepared to help all workers when needed
3. Stress giving the Lord the best
4. Help with teaching when called upon during the class period
5. Assist in planning all worship experiences

PRIMARY DEPARTMENT

Duties of the Primary Department Superintendent
(See Department Superintendent)

1. Be a good example of Christ before your pupils and workers
2. Constantly motivate workers in your department to improve their work
3. Cooperate with the other departments of the church and school
4. Stress the use of best methods in worship and teaching
5. Study the organization of your department
6. Stress attendance at workers' conferences and department meetings
7. Help workers make long-range plans for the work of the department
8. Periodically evaluate the work of the department
9. Take good care of facilities and equipment
10. Encourage all to take training
11. Be sure that there are adequate supplies and materials on hand
12. Represent your department in church meetings and business sessions
13. Conduct regular business meetings for your department
14. Make regular reports, when called upon, to the Board of Christian Education
15. Cooperate fully with the General Superintendent
16. Supervise the teaching process

Duties of Workers in the Primary Department

Primary Department Secretary

1. Keep all records of the department
2. Take roll and offering each Sunday without disturbing children and workers
3. Be ready to help other workers in the department when needed

Primary Department Pianist

1. Remember that you are also a teacher
2. Be prepared to help all workers when needed
3. Stress giving the Lord the best
4. Help with teaching when called upon during the class period
5. Help plan all worship experiences

JUNIOR DEPARTMENT

Duties of the Junior Department Superintendent
(See Department Superintendent)

1. See that your department is organized properly with sufficient number of classes, teachers, space, equipment and materials
2. Represent your department in all church meetings
3. See that the Junior program is coordinated with other agencies in the church for Juniors
4. Oversee the use of materials and equipment for your department
5. See that curriculum materials are ordered well in advance
6. Study and improve the record system
7. Stress the building of attendance in the department through recruitment of new members, surveys, use of mail, and visitation
8. Emphasize loyalty to the church
9. Encourage workers to be punctual
10. Plan a parent-teacher meeting at least once a year
11. Be constantly on the lookout for means of improving worship and study
12. Encourage workers to attend conferences and leadership training sessions
13. Hold regular department meetings (see Agenda under Department Superintendent)

Duties of Workers in the Junior Department

*Suggested workers for this department would include an Assistant Superintendent, Secretary, Pianist and Chorister. See Department Superintendent section for duties of these workers.

MIDDLE SCHOOL DEPARTMENT

Duties of the Middle School Department Superintendent
(See Department Superintendent)

1. See that your department is organized properly with sufficient number of classes, teachers, space, equipment and materials
2. Represent your department in all church meetings
3. See that the Junior High program is coordinated with other agencies In the church for youth
4. Oversee the use of materials and equipment in your department
5. See that curriculum materials are ordered well in advance

6. Study and improve the record system
7. Stress the building of attendance in the department through recruitment of new members, surveys, use of mail and visitation
8. Emphasize loyalty to the church and its purpose
9. Encourage all workers to be punctual
10. Plan parent-teacher meetings at least once a year
11. Be constantly on the lookout for means of improving worship and study
12. Encourage workers to attend conferences and leadership training sessions
13. Hold regular department meetings (see Agenda under Dept. Sup.)
14. Guard the teaching time of the teachers
15. Be zealous in the follow-up of absentees

Duties of Workers in the Middle School Department

*Suggested workers for this department would include an Assistant Superintendent, Secretary, Pianist, and Chorister. See Department Superintendent for duties of these workers.

HIGH SCHOOL DEPARTMENT

Duties of the High School Department Superintendent
(See Department Superintendent)

1. See that your department is organized properly with sufficient number of classes
2. Represent your department in all church meetings
3. Determine that the Senior High program is coordinated with other agencies in the church for youth
4. Oversee the use of materials and equipment for your department
5. See that curriculum materials are ordered well in advance
6. Study and improve the record system
7. Stress the building of attendance in the department through recruitment of new members, surveys, use of the mail, and visitation
8. Emphasize loyalty to the church and its program
9. Encourage all workers to be punctual
10. Plan teacher-parent meetings periodically
11. Be constantly on the lookout for means of improving worship and study
12. Encourage workers to attend conferences and leadership training sessions
13. Hold regular department meetings (See Agenda under Dept. Sup.)
14. Guard the teaching time of the teachers
15. Be zealous in the follow-up of absentees

Duties of Workers in the High School Department

Suggested workers for this department would include an Assistant Superintendent, Secretary, Pianist, and Chorister. See Department Superintendent for duties of these workers.

ADULT AND COLLEGE AGE DEPARTMENT
(See Department Superintendent)

1. See that your department is organized properly with sufficient number of classes, teachers, space, equipment, and materials
2. Represent your department in all church meetings
3. See that your department program is coordinated with other agencies in the church for adults
4. Oversee the use of materials and equipment for your department
5. See that curriculum materials are ordered well in advance
6. Study and improve the record system
7. Stress the building of attendance in the department through recruitment of new members, surveys, use of mail, and visitation
8. Emphasize loyalty to the church and its program
9. Encourage all workers to be punctual
10. Plan parent-teacher meetings periodically
11. Be constantly on the lookout for means of improving worship and study
12. Encourage your workers to attend conferences and leadership training sessions
13. Hold regular department meetings (See Agenda under Dept. Sup.)
14. Guard the time of the teachers for teaching
15. Be zealous in the follow-up of absentees
16. Set goals for your department

Duties of Workers in the Adult and College Age Departments

Suggested workers for the departments would be an Assistant Superintendent, Pianist, Chorister, Secretary, Librarian, and various assistants. See the section on Department Superintendent for a list of the duties of such workers.

HOME AND EXTENSION DEPARTMENT

Home Department Superintendent
(See Duties of Dept. Sup.)

1. Keep the morale of workers high
2. Cultivate individual "visitors"; become a real friend to each
3. Visit in homes of workers
4. Observe workers' birthdays
5. Show an interest in the department of each visitor
6. Be ready to counsel
7. Express appreciation for work
8. Visit in homes occasionally
9. Be familiar with materials
10. Keep posted on church affairs
11. Find workers for the department
12. Keep up-to-date list of prospects
13. Look for membership prospects
14. Train the workers
15. Conduct department meetings
16. Plan for expansion
17. Help plan social programs
18. Promote the department

Visitors

1. Plan carefully for visits
2. Pray much about your work
3. Have a clear purpose for visits
4. Take Bible with you on calls
5. Take materials to members for study and worship
6. When asked, teach lessons
7. Distribute tracts
8. Notify superintendent when absent
9. Be a friend and personal counselor
10. Call at convenient times
11. Share church news
12. Share good literature
13. Ask for envelope on offerings
14. Do not stay too long
15. Keep records and evaluations
16. Stress spiritual things
17. Keep records and evaluations of visits; make reports on them

Associate Superintendent

1. Be active only in a class with enrollment of 20-25 members
2. Preside in the absence of the Superintendent
3. Pool ideas for the benefit of all
4. Be in charge of new prospects
5. Give general assistance

Secretary

1. Feel importance of records
2. Set up records for members, prospects, workers, minutes
3. Notify staff about meetings
4. Instruct visitors in record system
5. Inform general secretary of work
6. Make reports on work of dept.
7. Take minutes
8. Order, distribute supplies
9. Report offerings taken
10. Receive reports from visitors

Assistant Visitors

1. Act as substitutes
2. Attend department meetings
3. Give occasional assignments

Extension Department

Very similar to Home Department. It does extend its work to elderly, ill, Sunday workers, and institutional people.

Correspondence Secretary

1. Visit people by mail
2. Contact military personnel, students and youth away at work
3. Send literature, news from home
4. Write letters to people away; urge them to relate to some church and Sunday School

DUTIES AND RESPONSIBILITES OF CLASS OFFICERS AND WORKERS

Purpose of a Bible Class

1. To teach the Bible
2. To reach all prospects
3. To enlist all prospects
4. To win all prospects
5. To develop Christians to pray, study, worship, serve; be good stewards; join in fellowship

Functions of a Bible Class

1. To help teachers
2. To train members
3. To develop members
4. To work effectively
5. To share responsibilities

Qualifications of Class Workers

1. Genuine Christian experience
2. Loyal church members
3. Love of the Bible
4. Love of people
5. Cooperation
6. Burden for unsaved
7. Willingness to work
8. Willingness to study
9. Growing Christian
10. Comprehension of the purpose of the class
11. Willingness to prepare for task

Duties of the Class President

1. Builds the administrative affairs of the class
2. Promotes the spiritual welfare of the class
3. Builds class spirit of cooperation, fellowship, service and evangelism
4. Plans and promotes outreach
5. Plans and promotes Bible study
6. Leads class in soul winning
7. Plans and promotes the spiritual development of the class
8. Plans and promotes the visitation program of the class
9. Encourages family worship
10. Creates an evangelistic spirit
11. Promotes Christian fellowship
12. Keeps class organized
13. Studies class records
14. Promotes excellence, promotes training
15. Promotes training program for the class
16. Plans, conducts class business sessions
17. Trains and improves self

Duties of the Class Vice President

1. Plans, directs social life of class
2. Creates genuine fellowship
3. Greets people for the class
4. Directs the class publicity
5. Makes classroom useful and comfortable
6. Protects class from unnecessary interference
7. Stresses excellence
8. Presides in absence of President
9. Takes assignments from the President
10. Takes training for himself
11. Studies his duties
12. Assists the President in class promotion

Duties of the Class Secretary

1. Knows and interprets the records system
2. Enrolls new members
3. Operates class system
4. Sees that records get to General Sec.
5. Cares for teachers' records
6. Reports class activities and records
7. Promotes use of records
8. Makes class information available
9. Trains an assistant
10. Studies his duties
11. Submits names, addresses of prospects
12. Reports absentees and late-comers
13. Requests, distributes supplies literature
14. Takes training himself
15. Serves as recorder at class meetings
16. Studies the literature
17. Attends all weekly class meetings
18. Attends workers' and prayer meetings
19. Is quick, accurate and enthusiastic
20. Helps the teacher take the offering
21. Helps welcome visitors and new members
22. Cooperates with Class President on publicity

Duties of Group Leaders or Captains

1. Promotes class spirit
2. Reports to Class President
3. Plans and promotes outreach
4. Takes personal interest in class members
5. Engages in visitation
6. Encourages personal and family worship
7. Leads members to Christ
8. Leads members to be good church members
9. Promotes stewardship
10. Promotes fellowship
11. Ministers to members and prospects in time of need
12. Uses record system information
13. Takes training for himself
14. Studies his duties and class literature
15. Stresses excellence
16. Directs class activities

Associates or Helpers

1. Takes assignments from officers to assist in class work
2. Helps in class work
3. Studies duties
4. Takes training for his work

Duties of Class Treasurer
(where separate office)

1. Keeps good financial records
2. Turns in collections and reports to church school office as soon as possible after class period gets started each Sunday
3. Deducts funds for class activities in accordance with class policy which should be explained by the Class President

Section Five

TEACHERS IN THE SUNDAY SCHOOL
Suggested Qualifications and Standards

I. **PERSONAL QUALIFICATIONS OF THE TEACHER**

    A. Faith
        1. Trust in God as Heavenly Father
        2. Trust in fellow men

    B. Virtue
        1. Pure
        2. Honest
        3. Courageous
        4. Grateful
        5. Desirous for the right
        6. Enthusiastic
        7. Industrious
        8. Economical
        9. Systematic
        10. Obedient
        11. Meek
        12. Joyful
        13. Consecrated

    C. Self-control
        1. Disciplined in all areas of life
        2. Stable
        3. Self-reliant
        4. Competent
        5. Penitent

    D. Patience
        1. Persevering
        2. Calm
        3. Cheerful

    E. Godliness
        1. Just
        2. Merciful
        3. Holy
        4. Forgiving
        5. Faithful
        6. Peace-inspiring
        7. Exemplary

    F. Brotherly Kindness
        1. Unselfish
        2. Gracious
        3. Courteous
        4. Helpful
        5. Thoughtful

    G. Love for God and Man
        1. Generous
        2. Reverent
        3. Loyal
        4. Affectionate
        5. Gentle
        6. Evangelistic

II. **QUALIFICATIONS FOR KNOWLEDGE**

    A. Knowledge of Christ
        1. Personal Experience
        2. Study and preparation
        3. Sharing with others

- B. Scriptures
    1. Facts
    2. Interpretation
    3. Application
    4. Other Interpretations
    5. History
    6. Archeology
- C. Principles of Teaching
    1. Set goals
    2. Teach pupils, not merely lessons
    3. Interpret the unknown by the known
    4. Use common language between teacher and pupil
    5. Relate to life
- D. Methods of teaching
    1. Practices
    2. Values
    3. Implications
- E. Psychology
    1. Age group differences
    2. Needs
    3. Interests
    4. Methods
- F. Students
    1. Family background
    2. School life
    3. Needs
    4. Strengths, weakness
    5. Home life
    6. Interests
    7. Accomplishments
    8. Spiritual level
- G. Life
    1. Natural problems
    2. Spiritual resource

III. QUALIFICATIONS FOR TEACHING

- A. Trained
    1. Personally prepared
    2. Emotionally prepared
    3. Spiritually prepared
    4. Intellectually prepared
    5. Practically prepared
- B. Disciplined Preparation
    1. Start early
    2. Study thoroughly
    3. Make lesson plans
    4. Pray
    5. Keep pupils in mind
    6. Define objectives
- C. Disciplined Presentation
    1. Follow plan
    2. Vary methods
    3. Make life application
    4. Apply principles
    5. Maintain interest
    6. Confront pupils with Christ
- D. Follow-up
    1. Visit pupils
    2. Make assignments
    3. Review lessons
    4. Clarify truth
- E. Improve teaching
    1. Study of books
    2. Conventions
    3. Continuous training
    4. Evaluation
    5. Workshops
    6. Observation of other teachers

DUTIES AND RESPONSIBILITIES OF TEACHERS

I. **THE TEACHER AND HIS WORK**

   A. As to Importance
      1. You are the pastor of your class.
      2. You can get closer to the individual than anyone.
      3. In teaching a class, you do greater work than performing a miracle.
      4. "He that winneth souls is wise."
   B. As a Christian
      1. Get right with God; have a clear, definite Christian experience
      2. Go on into the Spirit-filled life
      3. Have an earnest purpose to save souls
      4. Use the means of grace, such as prayer, almsgiving, church attendance, prayer meeting, personal devotions
      5. Exercise self-denial
   C. As a Church Member
      1. You should be a thorough-going church member. Put it first, and think it is the best.
      2. You should be an intelligent church member; know the history, doctrine and polity of the church.
      3. You should be a loyal supporter of the church, giving money, labor and influence to its support at home and abroad.
   D. As a Bible Student
      1. Take time for study
      2. Study the Bible itself
      3. Learn to think for yourself
      4. Apply the truth of the lesson to yourself
      5. Study the whole Bible
   E. As a Teacher – three ways to learn how:
      1. By observation; study successful teachers
      2. By practicing – learn to do by doing
      3. By reading books on teaching
   F. As a Pastor
      1. Be a safe example – "Like teacher, like scholar"
      2. Be a faithful friend – tell all of the truth
      3. Be a shepherd of the flock

II. **WHAT THE TEACHER NEEDS TO KNOW**

   A. He should know the Bible and its use.
   B. He should know related subjects, such as Bible history, geography and antiquities.
   C. He should know his pupils – age group characteristics, needs, personal life.
   D. He should know the laws of teaching.
      1. The Law of the Teacher – "The teacher must know that which he teaches."
      2. The Law of the Pupil – "The pupil must attend with interest to the lesson to be learned." – This depends on the following:
         a. Discover the pupils' planes of thought
         b. Guard against outside distractions

       c. Provide a lesson suited to the pupils' capacity
       d. Plan for the pupils' cooperation in the lesson
3. The Law of the Language-the language used in instruction must be common to both the teacher and pupil."
4. The Law of the Lesson – "The Truth to be taught must be learned through truth already known." Do this as follows:
       a. Review and connect with the previous lesson
       b. Proceed by graded steps, one step at a time
       c. Illuminate by illustration
5. The Law of the Teaching Process – "Excite and direct the self activities of the pupil and as a rule tell him nothing that he can learn for himself." Do this by doing the following:
       a. Provide thought material for him to think about
       b. Ask questions
       c. Get them to ask questions
6. The Law of the Learning Process – "The pupil must reproduce in his mind the truth to be learned, then express it in his own words." This is done in three ways:
       a. Reproducing the lesson – as by memory
       b. Interpreting the lesson – form own opinion
       c. Application – how to use what he learns
7. The Law of Review and Application – "The completion, test, and confirmation of the work of teaching must be made by review and application." There are three reasons for this:
       a. To perfect knowledge – repetition helps here
       b. To confirm knowledge – strengthens memory
       c. To apply knowledge

III. WHAT THE TEACHER SHOULD DO

A. Keep in training for your task
    1. Keep physically fit
    2. Be mentally alert
    3. Stay spiritually alive
B. Have a definite time and place for study daily
C. Have a definite object of study
D. Have a definite plan of study
E. Cooperate with all officers of the school
F. Attend all monthly meetings of the school

IV. WHAT THE TEACHER'S AIM SHOULD BE

A. To lead each pupil to a knowledge of God's will
B. To lead each pupil to an acceptance of Jesus Christ as personal Savior and Lord
C. To develop Christian character, which will be expressed through worship, right living and service

V. THE TEACHER AND HIS RELATION TO THE LESSON

A. How to study a Sunday School lesson – start very early in the week
   1. First, gather the materials
      a. Bible
      b. Lesson helps
      c. Good Bible dictionary
      d. Good concordance
      e. Pencil and paper
      f. Good commentary
      g. Maps, pictures
      h. Scrapbook
   2. Preview all lessons for the unit of study
   3. Read over the lesson in the Bible first of all
      a. Notice the subject of the lesson, and, as you read, meditate in the light of the whole
      b. Notice the Golden Text and the central thought
      c. Notice what book of the Bible the lesson is taken from; know something about this book such as the author, time, purpose, circumstances, etc.; you can find this in summary in the Bible most of the time or in one of the study tools
      d. As you read the lesson, write down the spiritual truths as you see them
      e. Ask such questions as:
         (1) What does the text mean?
         (2) What does the lesson as a whole teach?
         (3) What does the lesson teach in particular?
      f. Read it for the story
      g. Read it for the incidents
      h. Read it for the persons
      i. Read it for the teachings
   4. Then read the lesson "helps" in the light of your own study; see if your own thinking agrees with the commentary or writer of the lesson; thus, you have your view and his

B. How to prepare the lesson for teaching
   1. Ask yourself questions about the lesson
      a. What can I find that will meet some real need in the lives of my pupils?
         (1) Compare this with the stated aim of the lesson by the lesson writer; this gives you an aim for the lesson
         (2) Think about your pupils and their conduct
      b. Does the lesson teach faith, obedience, love, duty to God and man?
      c. Does it suggest Christian attitudes and grace?
      d. Does it encourage Bible study, prayer, etc.?
   2. Decide what the class needs and what they should receive from this lesson
   3. Next, decide what method of presentation to use; select more than one method of presentation to use, since the age of the pupils will determine this; if assignments are given, take time for them; then include question and answer time, as well as lecture

4. Do not try to present everything in the lesson; you will not have time
    a. Eliminate those things that don't apply to the class
    b. Select only material which will help you carry out your aim
5. If possible, arrange your lesson in outline form
    a. Make your own outline, if possible
    b. If not, follow the outline of the commentator
6. Provide for illustrations and applications under each point of your outline and questions
7. If pressed for time, stick to the main points
8. Formulate questions ahead of time and seek to formulate good applications to everyday life
9. Get your class to cooperate in the lesson
    a. See "How to use your class during the lesson" (Refer to E below)
    b. Make definite assignments

C. How to Teach the Lesson
   1. How to start the class
      a. First, welcome the pupils
      b. Pause for a few moments of prayer
      c. Refer to some topic of the day related to the lesson; tell a story or ask for reports of assignments
   2. Opening the Lesson
      a. Relate the lesson to pupil interests and needs
      b. Relate the lesson to the previous lessons
      c. Relate the lesson to the last lesson
      d. Then announce subject of the lesson today and how it fits in with what is being generally studied
      e. If wise, announce what your aim is
      f. Also, announce the general outline of the lesson you have made
      g. Read Scripture (See D. below)
   3. Developing the Lesson
      a. Develop the outline of the lesson by methods chosen through examination, illustration and application of the teaching materials
      b. Stimulate thinking on the part of the pupil
         (1) This can be done through carefully prepared questions
         (2) Also, it can be accomplished through telling a story
      c. Stimulate reproduction of the lesson by asking what the lesson means to individual pupils; give your own interpretation and application
   4. Closing the Lesson
      a. Sum up the lessons learned from the lesson
      b. Go briefly back over your outline
      c. Summarize briefly the conclusions of the class
      d. Ask if anything has been learned that will exalt Christ as Savior and show the need of Him as Savior
      e. Make life application
      f. Refer to the next lesson; try to whet the appetite of the class for the next lesson so that they will anticipate it
      g. Make any assignments necessary

D. How the Bible may be used in the lesson period
1. Lesson read by the teacher
2. Lesson read by one prepared pupil
3. Gist of lesson given in selected verses
4. References read at intervals
5. Fulfillment of prophecy
6. Promises underscored
7. Scripture quoted from memory
8. Questions answered by Bible verses
9. Lesson read in unison
E. How the class members can be used during the ,.lesson period
1. Tell lesson story
2. Conduct a quiz
3. Assign problems to be solved
4. Outline lesson board during discussion
5. Dramatize the lesson
6. Use a spelling bee for review
7. Assign opportunities to practice the truth of the lesson
8. Bring questions on the lesson; use a questionnaire
9. Share personal experience
10. Organize class
11. Let a member teach a portion of the lesson

VI. WHAT TO DO ON SUNDAY
A. You need to be present at least 15 minutes early
1. See that the room is in order; get nerves quiet
2. Greet your pupils as they come and look for needs
3. Plan pre-session activities carefully
B. Opening Assembly (if used)
1. Sit with your class
2. If your class has the program, join in
3. Take part in the services
4. Walk to your room with your class
C. Class period
1. This is your throne – use its power and influence
2. Organize to get things done
3. Stay on the beam and teach the Word
4. Teach for a verdict; do not be sidelined
5. Introduce all visitors and new pupils
D. Closing assembly (if used)
1. Sit with your class
2. Stress church attendance

VII. WHAT TO DO EACH MONTH
A. Be present at Board of Christian Education and workers' conferences
B. Remain for meeting with your department
C. Present your problems and suggestion
D. Always be ready for a report of your work

VIII. WHAT TO DO IN GENERAL
A. Attend church services and prayer meetings
B. Stay in touch with absentee workers

C. Visit the sick, careless and indifferent
D. Get the members of your class to visit; also use Visitation Day to get this done
E. Keep eyes open for new members
F. WALK WITH GOD; this is your biggest job
G. Be natural, friendly, cheerful, cordial, tender, patient, serious and enthusiastic
H. Be loyal to God and the church
I. Do not get discouraged; you are doing more than you realize
J. Cooperate with other officers and workers
K. Notify department superintendent well in advance if necessary to be absent or to resign.

NURSERY TEACHER RESPONSIBILITIES
(See General Duties of the Teacher above)

1. Be a dedicated Christian who is concerned with the telling of the story of Christ Jesus to pre-school children
2. See that the Nursery is adequately supplied with supplies and toys for the children
3. Create close relationships with the parents of the children, and attempt to solicit their help in the upkeep and supervision of the Nursery
4. Work closely with the General Superintendent in matters concerning the Nursery Department
5. Prepare your lessons diligently and thoroughly so that the children may get the most possible benefits from them
6. Attend all meetings where your department is involved as a representative of your department
7. Strive to keep up-to-date on the best method for teaching in your department, availing yourself of every training opportunity in both the local church and conference
8. Give a good testimony to your children in your attitude, conduct and words
9. Take an interest in the needs and desires of your children, and take an interest in their salvation, keeping this always in mind as the prime goal of both your department and those of the church school as a whole
10. Attempt to coordinate your teaching emphasis with the goals and aims of both your department and those of the church school as a whole

BEGINNER OR KINDERGARTEN TEACHER RESPONSIBILITIES
(See General Duties of the Teacher above)

1. Be a good Christian example for children to imitate
2. Be a growing Christian
3. Pray daily for your pupils and fellow workers
4. Cooperate with your Department Superintendent and other officers
5. Plan your teaching early
6. Arrive early to prepare for the teaching day
7. Greet pupils as they arrive
8. Be faithful in attendance
9. If you have to be absent, notify your superintendent in advance
10. Keep learning; read books; take training
11. Be flexible in your work schedule
12. Plan for pre-session activities carefully
13. Learn to tell Bible stories well; practice much
14. Plan relevant activities with spiritual value for beginner children
15. Lead the children in worship, in prayer, and in singing
16. Plan expressive activities for impressing Bible truth
17. Evaluate all class activities
18. Keep your room neat and attractive
19. Visit your pupils regularly

RESPONSIBILITIES OF THE PRIMARY TEACHER (Elementary 1,2,3)
(See General Duties of the Teacher above)

1. Take advantage of any teaching magazines which will inspire and help you
2. Pray that God will make you a channel of his love; remember each of your students, one by one, in prayer
3. Bring the scholar at the earliest moment into a conscious and intimate relationship to God as Father, to Christ as Savior and Friend and the Spirit of Truth
4. Present the claims of Jesus Christ to your students periodically, and give them the opportunity of making a decision to follow Him
5. Let the superintendent know early in the week if you cannot be present the following Sunday
6. Fill out the information on the front of the envelope
7. Set up a system within your class to check on pupils whose attendance is irregular
8. At the end of each month, give the Superintendent a list of those absent without a valid reason for two or more Sundays consecutively
9. At the first of each quarter, turn in all unused materials from the preceding quarter
10. Keep partially used books for visitors
11. Inform Superintendent of any additional materials you feel would be helpful
12. Emphasize the need of giving cheerfully and systematically to the work of the Lord
13. Make your room as attractive and interesting as possible
14. Keep shelves and cupboards orderly
15. Visit your pupils at home as often as possible
16. Plan interesting pre-session activities
17. Study and practice good story telling
18. Provide the children with opportunities to practice lesson truths
19. Stress Bible memory work with Primaries
20. Stress the plan of salvation in teaching
21. In singing, be sure Primaries understand word meanings
22. Conduct worship in terms of child experience

RESPONSIBILITIES OF THE JUNIOR TEACHER (Grades 4, 5)
(See General Duties of the Teacher above)

1. Be a mature Christian with an experience with Christ which you earnestly desire to share with your class members
2. Study your lesson thoroughly and be completely prepared for the teaching of your class
3. Attempt to be aware of other materials available to you, and try to utilize them in your teaching; some of these may be current events
4. At all times, encourage free discussion and the sharing of experiences of the class members
5. Be an example of a godly life to the children under your teaching
6. Be directly responsible to the Junior Department Superintendent, as well as being responsible to the General Superintendent of the church school on general matters
7. Take a personal interest in your pupils, knowing each one by name, and, if the occasion avails itself, call on these pupils in case of absence or special needs
8. Avail your self of any and all materials available for you such as media, Bible drills, memory verses, and other techniques especially good for use with the children of this age; you should become proficient in their use
9. Keep ever before you the ultimate goal of your teaching, the winning of souls for Jesus and the evangelistic thrust of the church
10. Attempt at all times to coordinate your teaching, first with the aims and objectives of the department you are in, and, second, with the goals of the church school as a whole
11. Be responsible for attending the department meetings as the leader of your class as well as any other meetings which you may be called upon to attend in your duties as Junior Department Teacher
12. Share the responsibility of planning for worship services preceding the lesson time (if used this way)
13. Study Junior characteristics in getting to know them
14. Visit in the homes of your pupils; find new prospects
15. Choose class officers and plan social activities
16. Study class records and stress attendance
17. Follow-up absentees
18. Arrive early; plan pre-session activities
19. If absent, notify the Superintendent in advance
20. Attend workers' meetings
21. Train yourself for your task

MIDDLE SCHOOL TEACHER RESPONSIBILITIES (Grades 6, 7, 8)
(See General Duties of the Teacher above)

1. Take plenty of time to prepare to teach; begin early and on time
2. Be clear-headed and warm-hearted; know you pupils; visit them
3. Keep pupils busy; plan pre-session activities and class projects
4. Encourage the use of Bibles; use various media
5. Primarily use the question and answer method
6. Use clear and simple aims
7. Use round table discussion
8. Do not be too impatient with movement because Middle School students are at a transitional period in life
9. Provide incentives such as Honor Rolls
10. Capture the leaders for help and leadership
11. Appeal to students as individuals instead of trying to drive the class as a whole; be enthusiastic; teach to meet life needs
12. Be thoroughly impartial
13. Organize the class with officers
14. Appoint committees such as social and visitation
15. Have a camp with them if possible
16. Cultivate the parents; follow up absentees
17. Do not be afraid to talk religion, but deal privately with them
18. Pray for your pupils daily
19. Take training; read much
20. Attend workers' meetings

HIGH SCHOOL TEACHER RESPONSIBILITIES (Grades 9,10, 11,12)
(See General Duties of the Teacher above)

1. Determine whether to have mixed classes according to the local situation
2. Have a class organization
3. Appoint standing committees
4. Try to give everyone something to do
5. Maintain a strong, Christian character
6. Have sincere sympathy for young people; study and know them
7. Do not embarrass students by questioning too much
8. Allow free discussion
9. Frankly admit your ignorance when necessary
10. Listen to reports
11. Prepare lessons early and thoroughly
12. Base all teachings on the Bible, not opinion; meet pupil needs
13. Be patient; visit your pupils; spend time with them
14. Cultivate an unfailing optimism and cheerfulness
15. Take training; read much
16. Attend workers' meetings

COLLEGE AGE TEACHER RESPONSIBILITIES
(See General Duties of the Teacher Above)

1. Prepare your lesson for the class thoroughly and completely, early in the week
2. Relate the lesson to the everyday life of your students
3. Organize your lesson in such a way as to bring about the best possible learning situation for your students
4. Be responsible to the Superintendent of the youth department in Sunday School matters, as swell as being responsible to the General Superintendent in all general Sunday School matters
5. Be responsible to the chaplains of the college age students in matters related to the teaching of your class
6. Be acquainted with your topic enough to know what you are talking about for the benefit of your students
7. Be creative and fresh in your approach in order to capture the imagination and interests of your students
8. Allow free and open discussion in your class, while not allowing the discussion to get completely away from the spirit of the lesson
9. Be a mature Christian with a genuine experience of salvation and a desire to share this experience with your students
10. Be an example of a godly life in word, in deed, and action so that your students will not be turned away from Jesus Christ
11. Take a personal interest in the needs and desires of your students; if the need arises, call upon your students in case of absence or a special need
12. Attempt to coordinate your teaching with the general aims and purposes of both your department and the Sunday School as a whole
13. Study and read; take training
14. Attend workers' meetings

ADULT TEACHER RESPONSIBILITIES
(See General Duties of the Teacher Above)

1. Be a mature Christian with an experience with Christ which you earnestly desire to share with your class members
2. Study your lesson thoroughly and be completely prepared for teaching your class; have a definite time, place and purpose for study
3. Be aware of other materials available to you, and attempt to incorporate them into your teaching; some of these may be current events, commentaries, personal experiences, etc.
4. Encourage free discussion and sharing and use class members; use a variety of teaching methods
5. Be a person of deep prayer and convictions, and accompany your lesson preparation with much prayer and meditation
6. Be an example in word, deed, and testimony to your fellow class members
7. Strive, except when humanly impossible, to be on time for the beginning of the class period
8. If you plan to be absent, see that a substitute teacher is engaged in plenty of time for that substitute to study the lesson properly

9. Take a personal concern for all your class members, striving to know them all by name, and, in case of special need or illness, attempt to call on that person and encourage him/her in time of need
10. Feel a call to teach and strive to share this calling with all class members
11. Be responsible for attending any meetings or workers' conferences in your department or in the church school as a whole as a representative of your class and your Savior Jesus Christ
12. Be responsible to the Adult Department in all matters within your department and to the General Superintendent in all general church school matters
13. Realize as your prime goal the salvation of your class members and the maturing of those members who profess to being Christian
14. Keep in touch with absentees
15. Visit the sick, careless and indifferent
16. Take training for your work

Section Six

WORKERS IN OTHER CHURCH EDUCATIONAL AGENCIES

Superintendent of the Weekday Kindergarten Program

1. Be a trained, spiritually aware, warm-hearted teacher
2. See that the school is run according to state regulations; have an accredited school if possible
3. Be aware of the statewide kindergarten program, and receive any help or aids that are available
4. Have sufficient facilities to begin a quality program; upgrade facilities according to the need
5. Have a well-planned program for children
    a. Allow time for religious emphasis
    b. Arrange for periodic programs which parents will attend
6. Create and continue good rapport with parents
7. Be interested in each child
8. Attend monthly meetings of the Commission on Education

Youth Fellowship Leader or Sponsor

1. Meet with officers of the Youth Fellowship to plan the meeting of the group at least three months in advance
2. Contact special speakers for the group
3. Be in attendance for the Sunday evening meetings, arriving early to greet the youth; know and love youth
4. Include recreation, singing, and a devotional in the church meetings
5. Plan and promote a fellowship time every other Sunday night after the regular evening church services
6. Plan and promote one big social event each month such as swimming, bowling, going to the movies, camping, hiking, or bicycling
7. Help the annual community drive: Heart Fund, March of Dimes, etc.
8. Cultivate spiritual and emotional maturity

Scout Leader (Applicable to Brownies, Girl Scouts, Boy Scouts and Cub Scouts)

1. Instill in your boys and girls feelings of patriotism
2. Instill in them a love for God and for His church
3. Attempt to build character in your boys and girls through service and example
4. Be an example to them in word, deed, and action
5. Cooperate at all times with the church and its leaders who are sponsoring the program
6. Be consistent with the Scout Handbook, which is the standard by which to measure your work
7. Attempt to bring about in your boys and girls a feeling of allegiance to the church
8. Encourage them to do much of their scout work, wherever it is possible, within the scope of church work

9. Strive to bring your boys and girls into a saving knowledge of Jesus Christ, if the opportunity presents itself

Institutional Representative for Boy Scouts

The Institutional Representative has three phases to his job:

1. Head the Scouting Department in the church
2. Serve as a Council member, a member of the overall governing body of the local Scout council
3. Serve as a working member of the district committee and, as needed, a member of one of its operating committees

The following is a list of detailed responsibilities:

1. Help recruit the right leadership
2. Encourage unit leaders and committeemen to take training
3. Promote well-planned unit programs
4. Serve as liaison between your units and institution
5. Organize enough units
6. Promote the recruiting of new boys
7. See that boys graduate from unit to unit
8. Assist with unit rechartering
9. Suggest Good Turns to your institution
10. Sit in on unit committee meetings
11. Serve as group chairman
12. Cultivate institutional leaders
13. Encourage active outdoor programs
14. Emphasize advancement and boy recognition
15. Bring in district help
16. Promote roundtable attendance
17. Invite commissioner service
18. Use approved unit finance policies
19. Encourage recognition of leaders

Institutional Representative for Girl Scouts

The Institutional representative is preferably selected from the church membership

1. Serves on troop committees
2. Has a basic knowledge of the Girl Scout organization
3. Acts as liaison between the Girl Scouts and the church
4. Places the girls in the troop of their choice, providing there is an opening
5. Helps recruit leadership for the troop of the church
6. Handles special projects as requested
7. Meets with the Scout officials pertaining to church requests
8. Meets with church officials pertaining to Scout requests
9. Arranges special recognitions with the church

RESPONSIBILITIES OF THE VACTION BIBLE SCHOOL DIRECTOR

1. Be responsible directly to the Commission of Education in all matters concerning the school
2. Begin planning for the school at least as early as February, preferably year-round
3. Be responsible for the selection of the best teachers and workers
4. Designate a person to head the publicity committee to properly publicize the school
5. See that the budget for the school is worked out in advance and approved by the Commission on Education
6. Begin in February to order sample supplies of Vacation Bible School materials from which to choose
7. See that the course is comprehensive, properly graded, coordinated with the total program, missionary minded, evangelistic, and simple enough for both teacher and student to grasp easily
8. As soon as it Is possible for the workers to get together (at least two weeks in advance), meet with them and make sure that all the arrangements are complete for the school; assign classrooms; plan special events
9. Arrange for a day of pre-registration in the church for the children to sign up for VBS
10. See that there is a time set aside for a dedication service for the VBS workers in the church service
11. Be in charge of supervising the arrangement of babysitters and transportation, if needed
12. Set an inspiring example for your fellow workers in the VBS as an able administrator and spiritual leader
13. Make sure that there are enough teachers and helpers in all departments to adequately teach the students
14. Strive to enlist the entire congregation in the work of the VBS through the ministry of prayer, transportation, and perhaps in the preparation of media and crafts before the opening of VBS
15. Arrange for an inspiring closing service with an evangelistic emphasis
16. Take charge of the follow-up procedure, attempting to see that all students are attending a church of some sort regularly
17. Make an evaluation of the school and supervise follow-up

DUTIES OF A CONFERENCE CHRISTIAN EDUCATION DIRECTOR FOR THE DENOMINATION
(Provided by Mr. Wayne Kenny)

Relationships
1. To the Superintendent – an assistant with authority to initiate and carry through conference Christian Education programs; to confer with the local churches in matters of importance to Christian Education; to report regularly to the superintendent, communicating progress, needs, etc.
2. To the Board of Administration – employed by the Board; ex officio member; report to the Board; advisor to the Board in matters of Christian Education
3. To the Board of Christian Education – Executive Secretary
4. To the denomination Headquarters – to relate the conference Christian education office to the General Christian Education office and to the Publishing House Christian Education Ministries; to interpret Denominational Christian Education programs to the conferences and Churches; and to interpret Conference and local Christian Education needs and opportunities to the General Office

Goals
1. To raise levels of performance in local Christian Education situations
2. To improve conference Christian Education programs
3. To improve cross-feeding between Sunday School and Youth programs
4. To increase enrollment, number, and quality of instruction in membership training classes
5. To increase the frequency of local and district Christian Education conferences

Duties
1. General leadership
    a. Initiate evaluative conferences with pastors, assistants, and General Superintendent
    b. Initiate and supervise conference projects and programs in Christian Education
2. Leadership Training
    a. Initiate teacher training on the local level
    b. Initiate membership training classes for all age levels
    c. Plan and execute area conferences in Leadership Training
3. Administration
    a. Administer the conference Christian Education program
    b. Initiate program planning for camps and conferences
    c. Supervise the local programs with the pastor and Sunday School superintendent
    d. Interpret conference needs to the General Office
4. Teaching
    a. Be available for private conferences
    b. Hold week-end conferences
    c. Do research in resources as needed
    d. Serve as curriculum consultant to local churches
5. Shepherding – encourage, interpret and strengthen local leaders

A GENERAL ANALYSIS OF THE JOB OF
YOUTH DIRECTOR OR EDUCATIONAL ASSISTANT FOR YOUTH
(Sample)

Relationship to the General Program of the Church
1. The Pastor
   a. Will work in cooperation with the pastor
   b. Will work under his general supervision
2. The Administrative Board
   a. Will be an *ex officio* member of the Administrative Board
   b. Will have full voting privileges
   c. Will, therefore, attend all meetings
3. The Council on Ministries
   a. Will be an *ex officio* member of the Council on Ministries
   b. Will have full voting privileges
   c. Will attend all meetings
   d. Will be the chief resource person of the program and policies for youth as set up by the Council on Ministries
4. The Commission on Education
   a. Will be *an ex officio* member of the Commission on Education
   b. Will have full voting privileges
   c. Will be the chief resource person on the program and policies for youth as set up by the Commission
5. The Other Commissions and Task Force Groups
   a. Will meet with the other commissions and task force groups where necessary
   b. Will relate the program of youth to the work of these commissions and groups
6. Youth Activities Beyond the Local Church
   Will help our youth be related to youth programs in sub-district, district, and conference levels

Relationship to the Youth in Particular
The Education Assistant in the area of youth will, of course, work closely with the Superintendent of the Study Program and especially the youth Coordinator in carrying out the directives of the Commission on Education and the Council on Ministries. He will confer with them regarding administrative matters and problems of the youth program. He will work with the Middle School and High School counselors in carrying out the directives of the Council on Ministries and the Commission on Education, the youth councils, the adult workers with youth, task groups, etc. He will have opportunity for creative study and thinking concerning the youth work.

   1. Evangelism
      a. Formulate and administer a systematic program for finding and recruiting people for membership in Youth division church school classes and evening youth fellowship
      b. Emphasize and plan for constant evangelism through the church school classes

      c. Give leadership in developing a broader and more thorough youth program in the areas of
          (1) Study – Bible study groups and youth prayer groups
          (2) Worship – effective worship services for youth in all worship meetings
      d. Make personal calls on young people for contact purposes, counseling, and cultivation – youth who are members of our church, church schools, or who are unchurched; goal of visiting every youth once per quarter
      e. Maintain complete records on all young people reached through program as to their church relationship and spiritual condition
      f. Help to execute plans for special spiritual retreats, weekend retreats, camps, outings, etc.

2. Recreation
After a careful and prayerful survey of the youth needs in this area in our church and community, he will outline and implement, with the help of adults in the church, a recreation program as extensive as is practicable.
      a. Athletic activities
      b. Parties
      c. Outings and retreats
      d. Clubs, etc.
        Keeping in mind always that every activity of the church, whether it be social, study, or worship, is a witnessing opportunity

3. Cultivation and Training
      a. Work with the Youth Coordinator in planning effective adult workers with youth meetings
      b. Work with each of the Departmental Counselors in planning and carrying out monthly council meetings for Middle School and High School youth separately
      c. Serve as consultant to teachers concerning their problems and plans and attend a different youth class every Sunday morning
      d. Plan and help to administer, in cooperation with the teachers, a program of effective absentee follow-up

4. Teacher Training and Recruitment
      a. Work consistently to discover teacher talent in the membership of the church, men and women, and recruit these people for prospective teachers and workers in the youth division of the church school
      b. Involve our youth and adult workers in training schools beyond the local church
      c. Plan a teacher-training program for in-service teachers and workers, either in a training school or make board use of the quarterly workers' meetings by Division; involve new workers in observation training at other local churches

5. Promotion
    a. Be responsible for establishing and maintaining a satisfactory and accurate record system for the youth church school classes
    b. Assist in the gathering of news relating to youth for the weekly church paper and perhaps do the same for a youth division newsletter

The Youth Program in Particular

Since this is the single area of particular responsibility for this person, there are certain things that need to be outlined:

1. The Youth Director will not necessarily assume any responsibilities now being carried by local people, i.e., teaching classes, etc.
2. He will serve as the chief administrator over the total youth program
3. He will train leadership, both adult and youth, in the youth division
4. He will serve as the chief counselor in the youth division
5. He will attend just as many youth meetings in the church of all types as is at all possible
6. He will be the chief coordinator of all youth activities
7. He will indirectly make contacts for and suggest programs and activity to the college-age group
8. He will use his own car without restrictions

DUTIES OF THE JUNIOR OR CHILDREN'S CHURCH DIRECTOR

This organization is a vital part of Christian Education in the local church. Many children who attend Sunday School never attend church, because their parents seldom attend. There is, therefore, a moral and spiritual obligation to provide these children with a worship experience in the Junior Church.

All classes which are scheduled to attend Junior Church should be present and on time every week. No pupil is to be excused or exempt from attending, if he or she attends Sunday School. Junior Choir members should also attend Junior Church services.

Each teacher and assistant teacher should sit with his or her class in Junior Church. By so doing, he or she will impress upon the children the importance of worship for them and will be able to correct any misconduct by members of the class.

DUTIES OF MEN'S ORGANIZATION WORKERS

1. To reach all men in the local church
2. To develop a meaningful faith and witness among men in all life relationships

Duties of the Men's Organization President

The President will preside at all meetings of the men, chair the executive committee, and assume leadership in developing a local program for men in keeping with the policies of the denomination.

DUTIES OF WOMEN'S ORGANIZATION WORKERS

1. To reach all women in the local church
2. To develop a meaningful faith and witness among women in all life relationships

Duties of Women's Organization President

The President will preside over a program geared to the needs and interests of women, and increase their concern for and knowledge of the responsibilities of the church in the world. She should share in Christian witness, service and missionary outreach, and organize funding for the program.

RESPONSIBILITIES OF MUSIC WORKERS

Music Director

1. Be responsible for all the music of the church and be chairman of the Music Committee
2. Prepare and direct assembly programs, including songs for worship and special music on special days
3. Provide pianists and choristers where needed; know musical talent of the church

4. Recommend suitable song books, and organize musical ensembles such as choirs and instrumental groups
5. On Sunday, come early; see that all song books are in place
6. Help with opening worship services
7. See that special music is provided where needed
8. See that announcements are made regarding choir practices, special music, special programs and publicity
9. Encourage children and youth to take part in the music program of the church
10. Be ready to assist with music in all departments; look for outside talent when needed; be ever on the lookout for improvements and new methods

Song Leaders

1. Chart your music for each service
2. Obtain suggestions from members, the pastor and other good sources
3. Help plan special music; select music
4. Keep music records; cooperate with church leaders

Choir Director

1. Plan music work with a committee and the pastor
2. Purchase good music; carefully mark and number music
3. Set up a music file
4. Conduct practices regularly

Choir Member

1. Work with your director and leaders
2. Listen and obey your leaders during practice sessions
3. Be on time for all practices
4. Sing unto the Lord

DUTIES OF THE SUPERINTENDENT OF TRANSPORTATION AND OUTREACH
(See Department Superintendent)

1. Supervise the personnel and program of the church's ministry; this will possibly include bus pastors, bus drivers, mechanics, and other workers enlisted, also substitute drivers
2. Plan, organize, advertise, and implement promotional emphases
3. Secure and distribute needed supplies for bus workers
4. Keep accurate, up-to-date records of the entire bus program
5. See that visitation calls are made at every home of a regular rider and every first-time visitor each week, either by bus pastors or substitutes
6. Maintain a list of available substitutes for the regular bus workers; in case of absence, fill a vacancy
7. Keep the church abreast of the present and potential outreach
8. Analyze the bus program; report monthly to the educational committee, alerting them to the needs and opportunities of the bus ministry
9. Upon consultation with the pastor and Sunday School superintendent, enlist workers for the bus ministry; submit names to the Board for approval and to the pastor for appointment
10. Report good prospects and special needs of route families to the pastor; send a list each week of first-time visitors to the pastor; keep him fully informed on the entire bus program
11. Conduct a meeting of the bus pastors each Sunday morning for receiving reports, discussing plans and needs, distributing material, and praying together
12. Lead the workers to realize the spiritual ministry they are performing in reaching people for Christ, that this is the most important business in the world for them; strive to promote a balance between all-out human effort and complete dependence upon the Holy Spirit
13. Participate in the regular weekly route visitation as much as possible, with a special emphasis on prospect calling
14. Visit with workers and ride bus as much as possible in order to familiarize yourself with the routes and people
15. Initiate and carry out a visitation program including the appointment of visitation workers upon consultation with the pastor and superintendent
16. Promote the visitation program, obtaining and distributing necessary materials for reporting

DUTIES OF TRANSPORTATION AND OUTREACH WORKERS

Bus Program Director

1. Be faithful in attendance, reporting necessary absences to the Transportation Superintendent as early as possible
2. Be conscious of time; arrive at the church at least ten minutes before the bus is scheduled to depart; leave on time, get to each stop at approximately the same time each week
3. Be friendly; know people by name; speak to them; maintain safety precautions; try to keep riders happy and occupied as they ride
4. Maintain accurate, up-to-date records; at each stop make a "p" for present or an "a" for absent for each person

5. Get information from visitors whether they wish to enroll as regular riders; if so, transfer names to route record sheet; give them enrollment cards
6. For visitors, fill out a visitor's card and place in visitor records; give a visitor card to each person to take to his department secretary
7. Maintain an up-to-date route map; note the location and arrival time for each stop; indicate with arrows the route taken by the bus; have route map and record book in order for use by substitutes
8. Duties at the church
    a. Ask visitors and others who need room location to line up by the bus
    b. Be first off the bus and make a head count as children leave the bus
    c. Take visitors to their rooms
    d. Meet with the Bus Program Director; make reports and suggestions
9. Departing from the church
    a. Be at the bus when the riders arrive; make a head count before leaving
    b. Make special announcements
    c. Return riders in the same order as they were picked up
10. During the week
    a. Pray for parents, children, and Sunday School
    b. Make a special effort to win people to Christ
    c. Make personal visits to the homes of a few riders each week (Saturday best day)
    d. At each home, leave a weekly paper (one per family) and make a quick call; if no one is at home, leave a note; record the visit in your record book
    e. Call on your visitors and new enrollees; find out if they enjoyed Sunday School and if they know of other prospects who do not attend church
    f. Look for prospects; watch for signs of children; ask children if they know of anyone who would like to ride the bus to Sunday School
    g. Fill out "enrollment cards" on prospects; give them information on how to ride the bus: location, time of arrival, etc.
    h. Win confidence and friendship of parents

Bus Drivers (responsible to the Bus Program Director)

1. Possess and maintain proper license (appropriate to size of vehicle, with proper passenger endorsements)
2. Arrive at the church at least ten minutes before scheduled departure time; check lights, tires, oil, and brakes before leaving
3. Start route in time to return to the church at least 15 minutes before Sunday School begins; plan your route so you arrive at the homes about the same time each Sunday
4. Drive safely, reporting any driving hindrances made by the riders to the Bus Program Director
5. Caution riders leaving the bus to cross in front of the bus and cross only after looking in both directions. Never leave the bus when riders are on the bus (If a breakdown occurs, send the Bus Program Director for help)
6. Be friendly and cheerful at all times; try to know riders by name and speak to them as they board and leave the bus
7. Report needs (such as bus repairs) and make suggestions to the Transportation Superintendent

8. Be faithful in attendance, reporting necessary absences to the Bus Program Director as early as possible
9. Be at the bus when riders begin boarding the bus for the return trip after church

DUTIES OF THE DIRECTOR OR SUPERINTENDENT OF TRAINING

General Duties

1. Cultivate a wide knowledge of people
2. Familiarize oneself with the total educational program of the church
3. Study good principles of church education
4. Take periodic talent surveys to discover potential workers (see sample survey in later section)
5. Set up an effective training program; this includes selection of workers, curriculum materials, time and place of training
6. Keep up-to-date records of all workers: their background, training, experience, and taking appropriate care of confidential information
7. Help to fill all vacancies in the workers' staff
8. Work closely with all supervisory personnel, such as DEC, pastor, church officers, and superintendents
9. Promote the training program, publicity and enrollment

Training Policies

1. Some type of leadership training program should always be In the church program.
2. Training needs to be provided for church officers, ushers, organization leaders, Sunday School and youth workers.
3. The selection of new workers to fill the vacancies created by resignations, moving, sickness, death, etc., call for a reserve supply of trained leaders.
4. Doctors, lawyers, salesmen, stenographers, etc., all train to maintain their efficiency; so should Christians who want to be more effective in their ministries as laymen.
5. Periodically, the church will provide training schools, workshops, and practical guidance to all workers in its program.
6. All workers are required to take training in the program provided.
7. Monthly meetings of departmental workers will afford opportunities for learning and sharing together; at times approved, teacher training specialists in specific areas of Sunday School work will present workshops in these departmental meetings.
8. See sample questionnaire ahead which might serve as a recruitment tool.
9. See sample workers' conference calendar ahead.

QUESTIONNAIRE
(Sample)

Recruiting leadership for the _____ Church

of _____.

Name _____

Address _____

City _____ State _____ Zip _____

Telephone
Home _____ Business _____ Cellular _____

Fax _____ Email _____

ART
___ I do art work
___ I do lettering
___ I do poster work
___ I do computer graphics
___ I arrange flowers
___ I am interested in decorating the church for special occasions
___ My hobby specialty is _____ _____

CHILDREN'S CHURCH
(During Sunday Morning Worship Hour)
___ Director or Superintendent
___ Teacher
___ Assistant
___ Pianist
___ Nursery attendant

(check preferred group)
___ 2½ - 3 year olds
___ 4 year olds
___ 5 year olds
___ Primary Church (grades 1-3)
___ Junior Church (grades 4-6)
___ Children with differences

HOSPITALITY
___ Will entertain delegates, conference personnel, etc.
___ Will open our home occasionally
　　___ prayer groups
　　___ youth groups
　　___ single young adults

KITCHEN AND DINING ROOM SERVICE
I am willing to assist in preparing
___ Food for church dinners
___ Refreshments for receptions
___ Refreshments for youth groups
___ Banquets or dinners for youth groups
I am willing to help
___ Plan a potluck meal
___ Set up and decorate tables
___ Serve as a waitress
___ Wash dishes with a group

LEADERSHIP – YOUTH SPONSOR
___ Would like to be a sponsor for youth
(check preferred group)
___ Middle School
___ High School
___ Single young adult

___ I have had experience leading groups
Details: _____
_____
_____
_____
_____

Other youth activities
___ Chaperone youth events
___ Be a youth counselor/mentor
___ Be a substitute leader
___ Other: _____
_____
_____
_____

QUESTIONNAIRE (p. 2)

MUSIC

I sing:
___ Soprano   ___ Alto
___ Tenor   ___ Bass

I am interested in:
___ Morning service choir
___ Evening evangelistic choir
___ Contemporary Praise Band
___ Other singing (specify):
_____
_____
_____

I play:
___ Piano
　　___ Read music readily
　　___ Could play when less difficult music is used
___ Electronic Keyboard
　　___ Familiar with chording from a lead sheet
___ Organ
　　___ Play pipe organ
　　___ Play electric organ
　　___ Feel qualified as an assistant only
___ Guitar
___ Percussion
___ Other instrument (specify):
_____
_____

　　___ Soloist
　　___ Ensemble

I can direct music
___ Lead congregational singing
___ Lead Contemporary Praise Band
___ Conduct the orchestra
___ Direct adult choir
___ Direct children's choir

Technical support
___ I can be music librarian
___ I can do PowerPoint presentations
___ I can turn overhead transparencies
___ I can operate sound equipment
___ I can operate/maintain computers

OFFICE WORK
___ Accountant
___ Bookkeeper
___ Data Entry
___ Computer
___ Willing to train on computer
___ Work on bulk mailings
　　___ Addressing with computer
　　___ Addressing by hand
　　___ Folding/stuffing/sorting
___ Sort/deliver Sunday School literature

RECREATION

I would like to direct recreation for:
___ Grade school youth
___ Middle School youth
___ High School youth
___ I enjoy planning games, etc. for children's parties/events

List sports you enjoy: _____
_____
_____
_____

I am trained in these sports:
_____
_____
_____
_____

SKILLS
___ Cabinet-maker   ___ Mason
___ Carpenter   ___ Plumber
___ Electrician   ___ Painter
___ Radio Tech   ___ Photographer
___ Auto Mechanic   ___ Seamstress
___ Practical Nurse ___ Interior decorator

List other specialties not listed above: _____
_____
_____
_____
_____
_____
_____

QUESTIONNAIRE (p. 3)

SUNDAY SCHOOL
I have had formal teacher training:
___ Bible school or seminary
___ College
___ Other (specify): _____
_____
_____

I have experience as a teacher of:
Age group: _____
Check preferred age group:
___ Preschool   ___ High School
___ Grades 1-3   ___ College Age
___ Grades 4-6   ___ Married Couples
___ Middle School   ___ Adults

I am particularly interested in:
___ Teaching
___ Assisting in teaching
___ Co-teacher
___ Coordinating a division
___ General Superintendent of S. S.
___ General Secretary for S. S.
___ Attendance secretary
___ Assistant attendance secretary
___ Literature and supply secretary
___ Missionary education for children
___ Memory work projects for children
___ Pray regularly for workers and pupils
___ Sunday School library

TRANSPORTATION
My car is available to transport people:
___ Sunday School
___ Worship services
___ Youth meetings
___ Youth parties, recreation, etc.
___ Other youth events
___ Other (specify): _____
_____

VISITATION
___ Call on the sick
___ Make nursing home calls
___ Do general visitation
___ Work on a visitation team
___ Help with community canvas
___ Visit Sunday School absentees
___ Visit in Sunday School recruitment
___ Have experience in personal soul-winning

WRITING
___ Editorial ability
___ Write poetry
___ Write plays or skits
___ Reporting for a paper
___ Have had experience in reporting
___ Knowledge of printing business
___ Am a published writer
___ Proofreading
___ Willing to lead a writer's support group

OTHER
In the space below, please write any other area in which you would like to serve the Lord and the church: _____
_____
_____
_____
_____
_____
_____
_____
_____

Section Seven

OTHER SUGGESTIONS FOR THE MANUAL

Supplies and Services (Sample)

The church shall provide supplies such as absentee cards, scissors, paper, scotch tape, crayons, etc. Notify your superintendent in advance if you wish to have supplies for the entire class. Church school teachers are reimbursed for the cost of necessary supplies which cannot be supplied by the church school. Copies of materials can be obtained from the church office.

1. Use of rooms for any function must be cleared through the church office.
2. Portable objects such as tables, chairs, media equipment or song books may be borrowed without charge for church-related activities, but this must be cleared through the church office.
3. Children's department supplies are available in the general cabinet; all unused materials, such as pencils, chalk, paper, etc., should be returned to the cabinet at the close of the lesson or when the class is finished.
4. Supplies for the other departments may be obtained from the Sunday school office.
5. All media may be obtained through the Sunday School office.
6. The church secretary will provide such services as typing, copying, and mailing for church workers.

Use and Care of Rooms and Facilities (sample)

1. Show appreciation by taking care good care of all facilities
2. Workers should arrive early; when you leave, see that doors are looked
3. Inspect your room upon arrival; see that it is clean and properly outfitted; if not, report this to your superintendent; leave the janitorial work to the caretakers
4. Try to leave your room as you found it...in good shape
5. Take good care of the chalkboards, bulletin boards, chairs and desks
6. Do not smoke

How to Order Supplies (sample)

1. In order to get supplies such as pencils, paper, etc., fill out requisition forms
2. Be as explicit as possible regarding names, grade, addresses, etc.
3. Be prepared to answer any questions regarding your order
4. Turn in your requests through your superintendent or leader
5. Allow at least two weeks' time for delivery; when your order is not available, you will receive notice

CHURCH SCHOOL FACT SHEET (SAMPLE)

Church school begins at _____ and dismisses at _____

Teachers and classes
1. Teachers should arrive early enough to greet members of the class and to ensure that room arrangement and teaching aids are in order and are present.
2. Teachers who must be absent on Sunday morning should contact their division superintendent in advance; his name is listed in the church directory; the Superintendent will secure the substitutes (except where there is a standing agreement between the superintendent and the workers regarding substitutes).
3. Rolls should be checked and offerings collected by _____.
4. Classes wishing to invite a guest teacher for a period of time must first contact the divisional superintendent who will get approval of the Commission on Education.
5. All class projects should be presented to the Commission on Education for purposes of planning and coordination.

Attendance
1. A person is enrolled in church school the first Sunday he attends unless he indicates he is a visitor.
2. No person should be dropped from the rolls without permission from the the Commission on Education.
3. Follow instructions closely to keep your record book accurate.

Literature

Good choice of literature is important. Church literature is varied to meet the needs of every church school class. Consult denominational brochures to get information on the coming quarter's materials. This will aid in ordering and in long-range planning. After selecting the desired literature, each teacher is responsible for submitting to the Chairman of Church Literature an order for literature each quarter. The chairman is listed in the church directory.

Supplemental Teaching Aids

A teacher has not only the opportunity but also the responsibility to utilize the church library and media resources whenever it will benefit the presentation of educational material. The teacher must be thoroughly familiar with the books, media, etc., that are available for use. Most church school literature recommends the use of additional reading and media. Some literature will contain filmstrips that can be coordinated with written materials. Purchases of additional books and media and rentals are coordinated by the Chairman of Church Literature. Computer software is helpful.

An invaluable service is also rendered to teachers by the Chairman of Media. This person will arrange to show a film upon request and have other equipment present at the time and place designated by the teacher. A teacher that wishes to use media should contact the chairman in advance. Under no circumstances should equipment be removed from the media room without supervision of the chairman who is listed in the church directory.

Workers' Conference

For training and business purposes, a Workers' conference should be conducted monthly. Such a conference gives workers opportunities to improve their work and to develop various themes in the church school calendar. See a sample calendar of a conference of this kind which follows on the next page.

Workers' Banquet

During the Fall of each year, an appreciation banquet is planned for all workers in the church education program. The purpose of this event is twofold: (1) to fete the teachers, staff, workers and administration and their spouses, and (2) to permit the workers to meet socially and be recognized for their work of the last year and to be motivated for the work of the new church year, thereby fostering open channels of communication, concern and mutual understanding concerning the Christian education program.

Open House

At some time during the church year the parents and friends of our Sunday School pupils are invited to come with them to meet the teachers and workers, see the learning process in action in the classrooms and in Children's' Church, and express their appreciation to the volunteer teachers for what they are doing in the area of Christian Education for their children.

This special day is successful in promoting better understanding and Interpersonal relationships between parents, teachers, workers, and students.

Promotion Sunday

Promotion Sunday is normally scheduled in this church in _____. (Here should follow a statement describing what is done on this day in your church.)

Other Suggestions for the Manual

1. Policies concerning organization
2. Description of award system
3. Registration policies
4. Use of the record system
5. Description of visitation policies and program
6. Description of the curriculum system
7. Expansion or remodeling plans
8. Budgetary items and policies
9. Bibliography and resources
10. Addresses
11. Promotional materials
12. Acknowledgements
13. Terms of office
14. Floor plans, attendance policies, and talent surveys (see questionnaire)

WORKERS' CONFERENCE CALENDAR (SAMPLE)

When?	September	October	November	December	January	February
What Theme?	Clinic Survey Report; Workers' Conf.	Leadership Training	Standards	Teaching for a Verdict	Membership Cultivation & Follow-up	Teaching Methods and Aids
Who?	Dr. Byrne, Chairman, Speaker	Mrs. Lindsay, Mr. John S. Skinner	Mrs. Lindsay	Dr. Coleman	Dr. & Mrs. Lewis	Mrs. Martha Moutz
How?	Survey Report copied; workers' manual projected	Explanation of teacher training 7:30-8:15 pm	Divisional meetings (first work on divisional standards)	Speak on Evangelism in the Sunday School	Description of work; Suggestions on follow-up	Puppet demonstration; Chalkboard lesson prep
Committees	Fellowship Supper Mrs. Kenner, Chairman					
Worship	Dr. Seamands 3 min.	Mrs. Lindsay	Paul Wood	Youth to Testify	Dr. Vogell	Yvonne Moulton
Plan Ahead	Teachers' Meeting Standards	Christmas Announce Teacher-Training Program	Finalize the Plans for Christmas Program Dec. 8?	Pray for Church Revival	Note change of Date for March	Note change of date for March
Division Meetings	Orientation business look ahead	Discuss Teacher Training methods	General Assembly to hear Division reports 8:15	Discuss Soul-Winning Methods	Discuss Follow-up system and visitation	How to use methods pupil participation
Commission Meetings	Comm. Divides and meets with divisions	None Divide into three groups	None Divide	Called Meeting	None Divide	None Divide

THE SECRET OF SUCCESSFUL SERVICE

To be most effective in practicing the demands of these job descriptions, church workers need to develop the best possible Christian character. We not only learn by doing, but also by being. We teach by being Christian.

In the next section of this work will be found suggestions on how to best live the Christian life and thus become fruitful Christian servants. The duties for Christian character development represent the ethical basis for Christian living and service.

SECTION EIGHT

THE DUTIES OF CHRISTIANS

Introduction

The Priority of Obedience

One of the great themes of the Bible is that of obedience. It is one of those words which summarizes the obligations of God's people. It is also a word which focuses on the duty of Christians specifically. It is important, therefore, for one to study the subject of obedience as revealed by the Scriptures.

From the beginning of mankind, the obedience to God became the test of character and one's true relationship to God. This is seen first in the story of Adam and Eve, when for them the test of their relationship to God as Creator was one of keeping His Word and obeying His commands. Obedience became the basis for God's blessing and their welfare. This is no less true for God's people today. For us, obedience forms the basis for God's approval and paves the way for God's help and benediction.

Good illustrations of obedience can be found in the lives of the great Biblical patriarchs. Abraham obeyed God's instruction to leave his home and go into a country he had never seen. His willingness to sacrifice his own son Isaac reveals his spirit of submission to God's will. Fortunately God stayed his hand in taking Isaac's life to honor Abraham's obedience.

The great Old Testament Patriarchs – Isaac and Jacob – obeyed God in bringing the great nation of Israel into being. Joseph obeyed God in resisting temptation and carrying out God's will in his life.

An outstanding example of obedience is to be found in Moses' life. Because he was open to God's will and guidance, God used him to deliver Israel from Egyptian bondage. Joshua followed God's leadership and was instrumental in the establishment of Israel in the land of Canaan.

Throughout the subsequent history of Israel, great judges and prophets led the people through hard times and instructed them in the will and ways of God.

Great kings, who were righteous, gave us some illustrations of the values of obeying God. Chief among them was David, a man after God's own heart.

Prophets great and small were constantly exhorting the people to obey God. Obedience meant God's blessing; disobedience meant God's displeasure. Daniel, the great prophet, obeyed God in the face of dangers and the threat of death.

In the New Testament, the disciples provided living illustrations of the blessings and benefits of obedience and doing God's will. We have the Gospels because they were faithful. By way of obedience, the great Apostle Paul became the apostle to the Gentiles and gave great Scriptures for our instruction.

Above all, Jesus Christ Himself is the supreme and greatest illustration of obedience. We see this in His life as a child when He was subject to God and to His parents (Luke 2:49-52). The writer to the Hebrews spoke of Jesus this way: "Though he were a Son, yet learned he obedience by the things which he suffered, and being made perfect, he became the author of eternal salvation unto all them that obey him." (Heb 5:8-9) The Book of Revelation reveals to us the great inheritance which is ours through our loyalty and devotion to God.

The Pressure of Duty

It Burns Like an Inward Fire
The prophet Jeremiah felt an inward fire that prompted him to perform his duty. "But his word was in mine heart as a burning fire shut up in my bones, and I was weary with forbearing, and I could not stay." - Jer 20:9

It Calls Like the Voice of a Lion
Amos felt impelled by duty to prophesy. "The lion hath roared, who will not fear? The Lord God hath spoken, who can but prophesy?" - Amos 3:8

It Binds the Soul to Its Task
Luke felt compelled to do his work. "But I have a baptism to be baptized with: and how am I straightened till it be accomplished?" - Luke 12:50

It Urges to Haste
John quoted Jesus as saying, "I must work the works of him that sent Me, while it is day: the night cometh, when no man can work." - John 9:4

It Makes the Message Imperative
The early disciples felt the pressure of duty in order to speak about the things of God. "For we cannot but speak the things which we have seen and heard." - Acts 4:20 (See also Acts 18:5; 20:22)

It Sounds a Woe in the Ears of Him Who Falters
Paul felt that he "must" preach the Gospel. "For though I preach the Gospel, I have nothing to glory of; for necessity is laid upon me; yea, woe is unto Me if I preach not the Gospel." - I Cor 9:16

The Example of Jesus
He felt the imperative call to duty. "He must be about his Father's business." - Luke 2:49
He must preach - Luke 4:43.
He must accomplish his work - Luke 12:50.
He must work while the day lasted - John 9:4.
He must go to Jerusalem to suffer - Matt 16:21.
He must obey the Father's command - John 4:34.
(See also John 14:31; 15:10; Rom 5:19; Heb 5:8; 10:9.)

The Example of the Disciples
Under pressure of adversaries, the disciples said, "We ought to obey God rather than men." - Acts 5:29
Joseph and Mary followed instructions - Matt 1:24,25; 2:12,13,19,20.
Paul was not disobedient to the heavenly vision - Acts 26:19.
The disciples followed Jesus - Matt 4:20; 9:9.
The disciples obeyed Jesus - Matt 2:6; 26:19.

Old Testament Examples
Noah – Gen 6:22
Abraham – Gen 22:2, 3

Joshua – Josh 11:15
Hezekiah – 2 Kgs 18:6

Christ's Teachings About Obedience
It is basic to character – Matt 7:24.
It is essential to membership in God's family – Matt 12:50.
It is the way to spiritual knowledge – John 7:17.
It secures the blessing of divine fellowship – John 14:23.

The Marks of Obedience

Action
"Be ye doers of the word and not hearers only." - James 1:22

Faithfulness
"Keep yourselves in the love of God, looking for the mercy of our Lord Jesus Christ unto eternal life." - Jude 21

Keeping the Commandments
Of Jesus – John 14:15, 21
Of God – Rom 13:8,9: Ten Commandments; Rev 14:12
Proves our love – I John 5:3; II John 6

Listening
Listen earnestly and obey – Heb 2:1-3
Leads to understanding, then action – Mark 7:14

Wholeheartedness
The children of Israel were expected to keep God's statutes with all their heart - Deut 26:16; 32:46.

Done Daily
The Israelites gathered the manna daily – Ex 16:21.
They read the Word daily – Neh 8:18.
They performed vows daily – Psa 61:8.
They prayed daily – Psa 88:9.
They were watchful daily – Prov 8:38.
We should bear our crosses daily- Lk 9:23.
We should exhort one another daily – Heb 3:13

The Results of Obedience

Abiding in God – John 14:23
Blessedness – Lk 11:28
Kingdom entrance – Matt 7:21
Kinship to Jesus – Mk 3:35
Knowledge of God – I John 2:3
Perfection of love – I John 2:5
Salvation – Heb 5:9

The Threefold Duty of Life

Appropriation

To take the cup of salvation
"I will take the cup of salvation, and call upon the name of the Lord." - Psa 116:13

To take instruction
"Take firm hold of instruction, do not let go: keep her, for she is your life." - Prov 4:13

To take advantage of life's opportunities
"So he called ten of his servants, delivered to them ten minas, and said to them, 'Do business till I come.' " – Lk 19:13

To take the water of life
"And the Spirit and the bride say 'come,' and let him who hears say, 'come'; and let who thirsts say, 'come.' And whoever desires, let him take the water of life freely." - Rev 22:17

Formation

After the divine plan
"And see to it that you make them according to the pattern which was shown you on the mountain." – Ex 25:40

A perfect example – Jesus
"For I have given you an example that ye should do as I have done to you." - John 13:15

Transformed life
"And be not conformed to this world, but be transformed by the renewing of your mind, that you may prove what is the good and acceptable and perfect will of God." - Rom 12:2

"And we all, with unveiled face, beholding as in a mirror the glory of the Lord, are being transformed into the same image from glory to glory, just as by the Spirit of the Lord." - 2 Cor 3:18

Danger of old ideals
"As obedient children, not conforming yourselves to the former lusts, as in your ignorance. But as he who called you is holy, you also be holy in all your conduct." – I Peter 1:14,15

Donation

With a free hand "Freely you have received, freely give." – Matt 10:8

Give or lose "For whosoever desires to save his life will lose it, and whoever loses his life for my sake will find it." - Matt 16:25

The blessedness of it "But in every nation whoever fears him and works righteousness is accepted by him." – Acts 10:35

As stewards of it "As each one has received a gift, minister it to one another, as good stewards of the manifold grace of God." – I Pet 4:10

The Whole Duty of Man

Fear God and obey Him
"Let us hear the conclusion of the whole matter: Fear God and keep His commandments: for this is the whole duty of man." – Eccles 12:13

Face judgment –
"For God will bring every work into judgment, including every secret thing, whether it be good, or whether it be evil." - Eccles 12:14

"And it is appointed unto man once to die, but after this the judgment." - Heb 9:27

THE DUTY TO DEITY

Introduction

Previously, the importance of obedience was stressed as a means of accomplishing our Christian duties. It is not, however, obedience for the sake of obedience, but the important key to this matter is "obedience to God." Following are some of the duties we owe to God as Deity.

To God the Father

We are to fear God (Reverence is included)
"Do not fear those who will kill the body but cannot kill the soul but rather fear Him Who is able to destroy both body and soul in hell." - Matt 10:28,

"Honor all people. Love the brotherhood. Fear God. Honor the King." I Pet 2:17

"Let all the earth fear the Lord; let all the inhabitants of the world stand in awe of Him." - Psa 33:8

"God is greatly to be feared in the assembly of the saints." - Psa 89:7

We are to glorify God

By praise - "You who fear the Lord, praise him." – Psa 22:23

By good works - "Let your light so shine before men, that they may see your good works and glorify your Father in heaven." – Matt 5:16

By fruit-bearing - "By this my Father is glorified, that you bear much fruit; so you will be my disciples." – Matt 15:8

By spiritual unity – "That you may with one mind and one mouth glorify the God and Father of our Lord Jesus Christ." - Rom 15:6

By entire consecration -
"For you were bought at a price; therefore, glorify God In your body and in your spirit, which are God's." I Cor 6:20

"Therefore, whether you eat or drink, or whatever you do, do all to the glory of God." - I Cor 10:31

We are to love God
- With all our hearts – "Jesus said to him, 'You shall love the Lord your God with all your heart, with all your soul, and with all Your mind.' " - Matt 22:37
- To patiently wait for Him – "Now may the Lord direct your hearts into the love of God and into the patience of Christ." - 2 Thess 3:5

We are to obey God – as profitable servants
- "So likewise you, when you have done all these things which you are commanded, say, 'We are profitable servants. We have done what was our duty to do.' " - Lk 17:10

We are to praise God
- In song – "Sing praises to the Lord, Who dwells in Zion." - Psa 9:11
- With musical instruments – "Praise the Lord with the harp: make melody to Him with an instrument of ten strings." - Psa 33:2
- Universally – "Let the people praise you, O God: let all the people praise you." - Psa 67:3
- Perpetually – "He Himself has said, 'I will never leave you nor forsake you,' so we may boldly say, 'The Lord is my helper, I will not fear; what can man do to me?' " - Heb 13:5,6
- Why? - We are a royal priesthood. We are a chosen generation. We are a holy nation. We are a special people. - I Pet 2:9

We are to remember God
- In the battles of life – "And I looked, and arose and said to the nobles, to the leaders, and to the rest of the people, 'Do not be afraid of them, remember the Lord, great and awesome, and fight for your brethren, your sons, your daughters, your wives, and your houses.' " - Neh 4:14
- In the night season – "When I remember you on my bed, I meditate on you in the night watches." - Psa 63:6
- In early life - "Remember now your creator in the days of your youth." – Eccles 12:1
- In times of trouble – "When my soul fainted within me, I remembered the Lord." - Jonah 2:7
- When away from home – "I will sow them among the peoples, and they shall remember me in far countries." - Zech 10:9
- We are to act as remembrances
    - Timothy – I Tim 4:16
    - Peter – I Pet 1:12

We are to seek God
- In prayer – "And I say to you, ask and it will be given to you; seek, and you will find." - Lk 11:10
- To enjoy Him – "They should seek the Lord, in the hope that they might grope for Him and find Him, though He is not far from each of us." - Acts 17:27

We are to submit to God – to His divine will
- "Your kingdom come, your will be done." - Matt 6:10
- By service – "Then Mary said, 'Behold the maidservant of the Lord: Let it be to me according to your word.' " - Lk 1:38
- By yielding ourselves - "God be thanked that though you were slaves of sin, yet you obeyed from the heart that form of doctrine to which you were delivered." – Rom 6:17

By transformed living – "I beseech you, therefore, brethren, by the mercies of God, that you present your bodies a living sacrifice, holy, acceptable to God, which is your reasonable service, and be not conformed to this world, but be transformed by the renewing of your mind, that ye may prove what is that good and perfect will of God." - Rom 12:1,2

By resisting the devil – "Therefore submit to God. Resist the devil and he will flee from you." - Jas 4:7

By valuing Him above all – "Not everyone that says to me, 'Lord, Lord,' shall enter the kingdom of heaven, but he who does the will of my Father in heaven." - Matt 7:21

By establishing a divine relationship – "For whosoever does the will of my Father in heaven is my brother and sister and mother." - Matt 12:50

By obtaining spiritual knowledge – "If anyone wants to do His will, he shall know concerning the doctrine, whether it is from God or whether I speak of my own authority." - John 7:17

This is the rule of everyday life – "You ought to say, 'if the Lord wills, we shall live and do this or that.' " - Jas 4:15

We are to worship God

With our whole heart – "As servants of Christ, doing the will of God from the heart." - Eph 6:6

Because He is the only worthy one – "You shall worship the Lord your God, and Him only you shall serve." - Matt 4:10

Because He is a Spirit – "God is a Spirit, and those who worship Him must worship in spirit and truth." - John 4:24

Because He is the divine Sovereign over all – "Worship Him Who made heaven and earth, the sea and springs of water." - Rev 14:7

To God the Son, Jesus Christ

The disciples obeyed Jesus

"Then they immediately left their nets and followed Him." - Matt 4:20

"So the disciples went and did as Jesus commanded them." - Matt 22:6

We should obey Jesus

"Whoever comes to me, and hears my sayings and does them, I will show whom he is like." - Lk 6:47

"Teaching them to observe all things that I have commanded you." - Matt 28:20

We should love Jesus

"If ye love me, keep my commandments." - John 14:15

"He who has my commandments and keeps them, it is he who loves me." "If anyone loves me, he will keep my words." - John 14:21,23

We should learn from Him

"Take my yoke upon you and learn from me, for I am gentle and lowly in heart, and you will find rest for your souls." - Matt 11:29

We should deny ourselves and take up our cross

"If anyone desires to come after me, let him deny himself and take up his cross, and follow me." – Matt 16:24

We should abide in Him

"I am the vine, ye are the branches. He who abides in me, and I in him, bears much fruit, for without me ye can do nothing." – John 15:5

We should confess him
"Therefore whoever confesses me before men, him will I also
confess before my Father Who is in heaven." - Matt 10:32

"If you confess with your mouth the Lord Jesus and believe in
your heart that God has raised Him from the dead, you will be
saved." - Rom 10:9

We should have faith in Him
"For God so loved the world that He gave His only begotten
Son, that whoever believes in Him should not perish but have
everlasting life." - John 3:16

"These are written that you may believe that Jesus is the
Christ, the Son of God, and that believing you may have life
In His name." - John 20:31

We should be loyal to Him
"For whoever is ashamed of me and my words, of him the Son of
Man will be ashamed when He comes in his own glory." – Lk 9:26

We should be willing to suffer for Him
Willing to be persecuted
"Blessed are you when they revile and persecute you, and say all
kinds of evil against you falsely for my sake." – Matt 5:11

Willing to be hated
"And you will be hated for my name's sake, but he who endures
to the end will be saved." –Matt 10:22

Willing to lose life
"He who finds his life will lose it, and he who loses his life for my
sake will find it." – Matt 10:39

We should be willing to renounce worldly treasures
"And everyone who has left houses or brothers or sisters or father or
mother or wife or children or lands, for my name's sake, shall
receive a hundredfold, and inherit everlasting life." – Matt 19:29

We should be willing to lose our reputation
"We are fools for Christ's sake, but you are wise in Christ." – I Cor 4:10

We should be willing to die for Him
"For we who live are always delivered to death for Jesus' sake, that the
life of Jesus also may be manifested In our mortal flesh."
- II Cor 4:11

To God the Holy Spirit

Believers are to witness in His power
"You shall receive power when the Holy Spirit has come upon you, and
you shall be witnesses to me in Jerusalem, and in all Judea and
Samaria, and to the end of the earth." – Acts 1:8

Believers should ask for Him
"If you then, being evil, know how to give good gifts to your children, how
much more will your heavenly Father give the Holy Spirit to those
who ask Him." – Lk 11:13

Believers should follow His teachings
"The Helper, the Holy Spirit, whom the Father will send in my name, He will
teach you all things, and bring to your remembrance all
things that I said to you." – John 14:26

Believers should follow His leadership
By seeking His guidance
"When He, the Spirit of Truth, has come He will guide you into all truth." - John 16:13
"When they had gone through Phrygia, and the region of Galatia, they were forbidden by the Holy Spirit to preach the Word in Asia." - Acts 16:6
By submitting to His control
"While Peter thought about the vision, the Spirit said to him, 'Behold, three men are seeking you. Arise therefore go down and go with them, doubting nothing, for I have sent them.' " – Acts 10:19,20

Obedience to Him, a mark of sonship
"As many as are led by the Spirit of God, these are sons of God." – Rom 8:14

He will guide us
"When He, the Spirit of Truth has come, He will guide you into all truth." – John 16:13

PERSONAL AND INDIVIDUAL DUTIES

Introduction

The Scriptures not only give the general principles and directions for observing the priority of obedience and duties to Deity, but they also provide very specific revelation about personal and individual duties. What we ought to do is given specific meaning in the actions we take and the attitudes we manifest in our daily Christian living. Furthermore, the Scriptures outline explicitly what the believer's walk should look like.

Actions

Principles of Performance

Working in the light
"I must work the works of Him who sent me while it is day, for the night is coming when no man can work."– John 9:4

Warring in the light
"The night is far spent, the day is at hand. Therefore, let us cast off the works of darkness, and let us put on the armor of light." – Rom 13:12

Walking in the light
"For you were once darkness, but now you are light in the Lord. Walk as children of light." – Eph 5:8

Witnessing in the light
"You may become blameless and harmless, children of God without fault in the midst of a crooked and perverse generation, among whom you shine as lights in the world." – Phil 2:15

Watching in the light
"You are all sons of light and sons of the day. We are not of the night nor of darkness. Therefore, let us not sleep as others do, but let us watch and be sober." – I Thess 5:5,6

Priorities to Observe

Strive for perfection
"You shall be perfect, just as your Father in heaven is perfect." – Matt 5:48
Seek first the Kingdom
"Seek first the kingdom of God and His righteousness, and all these things shall be added to you. Therefore, do not worry about tomorrow, for tomorrow will worry about its own things. Sufficient for the day is its own trouble." - Matt 6:33, 34
Do all in His name
"And whatever you do in word or deed, do all in the name of the Lord Jesus, giving thanks to God the Father through Him." – Col 3:17
Do everything heartily
"Whatever you do, do it heartily, as to the Lord and not to man." – Col 3:23
Be diligent to make your calling sure
"Therefore, brethren, be even more to make your calling and election sure." – 2 Pet 1:10
Keep out of debt
"Owe no one anything except to love one another, for he who loves another has fulfilled the Law." – Rom 13:8

Practices to Carry Out

Charitableness
"We then who are strong ought to bear with the scruples of the weak, and not please ourselves." Rom 15:1
"Brethren, if any man be overtaken in a trespass, you who are spiritual restore such a one in a spirit of gentleness, considering yourself lest you also be tempted." - Gal 6:1
Fruitfulness
"By this my Father is glorified, that you bear much fruit, so you will be my disciples." - John 15:8
"You did not choose me, but I chose you and appointed you that you should go and bear fruit." John 15:16
"Walk worthy....being fruitful in every good work." Gal 1:10
Goodness
"I say to you, love your enemies, bless those who curse you, do good to those who hate you, and pray for those who spitefully use you and persecute you." - Matt 5:44
"Do not be overcome by evil, but overcome evil with good." - Rom 12:21
Hearing
"If anyone has ears to hear, let him hear." - Mk 4:23
"My beloved brethren, let every man be swift to hear, slow to speak, slow to wrath." - Jas 1:19

Purity
"Blessed are the pure in heart, for they shall see God." - Matt 5:8
"Now the purpose of the commandment is love from a pure heart." - I Tim 1:5
"Therefore having these promises, beloved, let us cleanse ourselves from all filthiness of the flesh and spirit, perfecting holiness in the fear of God." - II Cor 7:1

Retaliation
"I tell you not to resist an evil person, but whoever slaps you on your right cheek, turn the other to him also." - Matt 5:39
"Repay no one evil for evil." - Rom 12:17
"Beloved, do not avenge yourselves, but rather give place to wrath, for it is written, 'Vengeance is mine, I will repay, says the Lord.' " - Rom 12:19

Separation
From the lusts of the flesh
"Put on the Lord Jesus Christ, and make no provision for the flesh, to fulfill its lusts." - Rom 13:14
"Put to death your members which are on the earth: fornication, uncleanness, passion, evil desire, and covetousness." - Col 3:5
From the works of darkness
"Have no fellowship with the unfruitful works of darkness, but rather expose them." – Eph 5:11
From all evil
"Abstain from every form of evil." - Thess 5:22
"Do not let sin reign in your mortal body, that you should obey it in its lusts. And do not present your members as instruments of unrighteousness to sin, but present yourselves to God, as being alive from the dead, and your members as instruments of righteousness to God." - Rom 6:12, 13
"Now you must put off all these: anger, wrath, malice, blasphemy, filthy language out of your mouth." - Col 3:8

Speech
We are not to swear
"But I say to you, do not swear at all." – Matt 5:34
We are to speak the good
"Let no corrupt communication proceed out of your mouth, but what is good for necessary edification, that it may impart grace to the hearers." – Eph 4:29

Control the Tongue- Read James 3:1-12
"If anyone among you thinks he is religious, and does not control his tongue but deceives his own heart, this one's religion is useless." - Jas 1:26

Seasoned Speech
"Let your speech always be with grace, seasoned with salt, that ye may know how you ought to answer each one." – Col 4:6

Steadfastness
"My beloved brethren, be steadfast, unmovable, always abounding in the work of the Lord, knowing that your labor is not in vain in the Lord." – I Cor 15:58

In enduring hardship
> "You shall be hated by all for my name's sake. But he that endures to the end will be saved." – Matt 10:22

In persevering to the end
> "Since we are surrounded by so great a cloud of witnesses, let us lay aside every weight, and the sin which so easily ensnares us, and let us run with endurance the race that is set before us." – Heb 12:1

In moving forward
> "Jesus said to him, 'No one, having put his hand to the plow, and looking back, is fit for the Kingdom of God.' " – Lk 9:62

In establishing a Christian walk
> "As you have therefore received Christ Jesus the Lord, so walk in Him, rooted and built up In Him and established in the faith." – Col 2:6,7

In holding fast the faith
> "Seeing then that we have a great High Priest Who has passed through the heavens, Jesus the Son of God, let us hold fast our confession." – Heb 4:14

Suffering for Christ's sake
> "If children, then heirs...heirs of God and joint heirs with Christ, if indeed we suffer with Him, that we may also be glorified together." – Rom 8:17

Swearing

Profanity should be avoided
> "Above all, my brethren, do not swear, either by heaven, or by earth, or with any other oath." – Jas 5:12

Bless those who curse us
> "Bless those who persecute you; bless and do not curse." – Rom 12:14

Temperance

No strong drink for brother's sake
> "It is good neither to eat meat nor drink wine nor do anything by which your brother stumbles or is offended or made weak." – Rom 14:21

Control over the spirit
> "He who is slow to anger is better than the mighty, and he who rules his spirit than he who takes a city." – Prov 16:32

Control over life
> "Now as he (Paul) reasoned about righteousness, self-control, and the judgment to come, Felix was afraid and answered, 'Go away for now, when I have a convenient time I will call for you.' " – Acts 24:25

Control over lusts of the flesh
> "Do not let sin reign in your mortal body, that you should obey it in its lusts." – Rom 6:12

Control over the tongue
> "If any does not stumble in word, he Is a perfect man, able also to bridle the whole body." – Jas 3:2

A cardinal virtue
> "Giving all diligence, add to your faith virtue, to virtue knowledge, to knowledge self-control." – 2 Peter 1:5,6

Work
- Work at good things
  - "Let him that stole steal no longer, but rather let him labor, working with his hand what is good that he may have something to give him who has need." – Eph 4:28
- Be diligent
  - "Beloved, looking forward to these things, be diligent to be found by Him in peace, without spot and blameless." – 2 Peter 3:14
- Be industrious
  - "Not lagging in diligence, fervent in spirit, serving the Lord." – Rom 12:11
- Cooperate with God
  - "We are God's fellow workers." – I Cor 3:9
- Give immediate service
  - "A man had two sons, and he came to the first sand said, 'Son, go, work today in my vineyard.' " – Matt 21:28
- Work abundantly
  - "My beloved brethren, be steadfast, immovable, always abounding in the work of the Lord, knowing that your labor is not in vain in the Lord." – I Cor 15:58
- Work should be finished
  - "I have fought a good fight, I have finished the race, I have kept the faith." – 2 Tim 4:7

Zeal
- For spiritual development
  - "Even so, since you are zealous for spiritual gifts, let it be for edification of the church that you speak to excel." – I Cor 14:12
- For soul saving
  - "Behold I say to you, lift up your eyes and look at the fields, for they are already white for the harvest." – John 4:35
- For service
  - "Be always abounding in the work of the Lord." – I Cor 15:58

Attitudes

Anger

Swiftly get rid of anger
"Be angry and do not sin; do not let the sun go down on your wrath." – Eph 4:26

Be slow to wrath
"Let every man be swift to hear, slow to speak, slow to wrath." – Jas 1:19

Boldness

Toward Christ
"According to the eternal purpose which He accomplished in Christ Jesus our Lord, in whom we have boldness and access with confidence through faith in Him." – Eph 3:11, 12

To come to the throne
"Let us therefore come boldly to the throne of grace that we may obtain mercy and find grace to help in time of need." – Heb 4:16

To face the judgment
"Love has been perfected among us in this: that we may have boldness in the day of judgment; because as He is, so are we in this world." – I John 4:17

Carelessness

Leads to disobedience
"Now everyone who hears these sayings of mine, and does not do them, will be like a foolish man who built his house on the sand." – Matt 7:26

Leads to shallowness
"When anyone hears the word of the kingdom, and does not understand it, then the wicked one comes and snatches away what was sown in the heart." – Matt 13:19

Leads to hardness
"But He said to him, 'If they do not hear Moses and the Prophets, neither will they be persuaded though one rise from the dead.' " – Luke 16:31

Cheerfulness

Because Jesus has overcome the world
"Be of good cheer, I have overcome the world." – John 16:33

Because God will keep His word
"Take heart, men, I believe God that it will be just as it was told me." – Acts 27:25

Compassion

Helpfulness
"I have shown you in every way, by laboring like this, that you must support the weak." – Acts 20:35

Burden-bearing
"We then who are strong ought to bear with the scruples of the weak, and not to please ourselves." – Rom 15:1

Visit of the needy
"Pure and undefiled religion before God and the Father is this: to visit orphans and widows in their trouble, and to keep oneself unspotted from the world." – Jas 1:27

Earnestness

In love
"Jesus said to him, 'You shall love the Lord your God with all your heart, with all your soul, and with all your mind. This is the first and great commandment.' " – Matt 22:37, 38

In obedience
"Because He has inclined his ear to me therefore I will call upon Him as long as I live." Psalm 116:2

"Blessed are those who keep his testimonies, who seek Him with the whole heart." - Psalm 119:2

In trust
"Trust in the Lord with all your heart and lean not on your own understanding." – Prov 3:5

In prayer
"You will seek me and find me when you search for me with all your heart." – Jer 29:13

In repentance
"Phillip said, 'If you believe with all your heart, you may (be baptized).' " – Acts 8:37

In consecration
"I beseech you therefore, brethren, by the mercies of God, that you present your bodies a living sacrifice, holy, acceptable to God, which is your reasonable service." – Rom 12:1

Favor

Renders life secure
"When a man's ways please the Lord he makes even his enemies to be at peace with him." – Prov 16:7

Special duty to please God
"Brethren we urge and exhort in the Lord Jesus that you should abound more and more, just as you received from us how you ought to walk and please God." – I Thess 4:1

Be benevolent
"Do not forget to do good and to share, for with such sacrifices God is well pleased." – Heb 13:16

Forbearance

Bear all things
(Love) "bears all things." – I Cor 13:7

Forgive one another
(Beloved) "bearing with one another, and forgiving one another." – Col 3:13

Forgiveness

Obtained through confession of sin
"If we confess our sins, He is faithful and just to forgive us our sins and to cleanse us from all unrighteousness." – I John 1:9

Forgive others without limits
"And if he sins against you seven times in a day, and seven times in a day returns to you, saying, 'I repent,' you shall forgive him." – Lk 17:4
Forgiving others leads to divine forgiveness
"And whenever you stand praying, if you have anything against anyone, forgive him, that your Father in heaven may also forgive you your trespasses, but if you do not forgive, neither will your Father in heaven forgive your trespasses." - Mk 11:25, 26

Gentleness

Servants of God must not strive
"The servant of the Lord must not quarrel, but be gentle to all." – II Tim 2:24
They should be gentle to others
"Speak evil of no one…be peaceable, gentle, showing all humility to all men." – Tit 3:2

Humility

Secret to greatness
"Whoever humbles himself as this little child is the greatest in the kingdom of heaven." – Matt 18:4
Secret to good thinking
"I say through the grace that is given to me, to everyone who is among you, not to think of himself more highly than he ought to think, but to think soberly, as God has dealt to each one a measure of faith." – Rom 12:3
Secret to God's approval
"Humble yourselves in the sight of the Lord, and He will lift you up." – Jas 4:10
Leads to ultimate exaltation
"Humble yourselves under the mighty hand of God, that He may exalt you in due time." – I Pet 5:6

Loyalty

To the nation by paying taxes
(Jesus said) " 'Show me the tax money.' So they brought him a denarius. And he said to them, 'Whose image and inscription is this?' They said to Him, 'Caesar's.' And He said to them, "Render, therefore to Caesar the things that are Caesar's, and to God the things that are God's.' " – Matt 22:19-21
To government authority
"Let every soul be subject to the government authorities." – Rom 13:1
To give good example
"Submit yourselves to every ordinance of man for the Lord's sake…and for the praise of those who do good." – I Pet 2:13, 14
To contend for the faith
"I found it necessary to write to you…to contend earnestly for the faith which was once for all delivered to the saints." – Jude 3

Meekness

Be non-resistant
"To him who strikes you on the one cheek, offer the other also. And from him who takes away your cloak, do not withhold your tunic either." – Luke 6:29

Bear fruit of the Spirit
"The fruit of the Spirit is love, joy, peace, longsuffering, kindness, goodness, faithfulness, gentleness, self-control. Against such there is no law." – Gal 5:22, 23

Teach that it is essential
"Be gentle to all, able to teach, patient, in humility correcting those who are in opposition." – II Tim 2:24, 25

Instruct that it must be heard
"Lay aside all filthiness and overflow of wickedness, and receive with meekness the implanted word, which is able to save your souls." – Jas 1:21

Show that it is precious in God's sight
"Let it be the hidden person of the heart, with the incorruptible ornament of a gentle and quiet spirit, which is very precious in the sight of God." – I Pet 3:4

Patience

In tribulation
"Rejoicing in hope, patient in tribulation, continuing steadfastly in prayer." – Rom 12:12

In leading to perfection
"Let patience have its perfect work that you may be perfect and complete, lacking nothing." – Jas 1:4

In waiting for Jesus' return
"Be patient, brethren, until the coming of the Lord. See how the farmer waits for the precious fruit of the earth, waiting patiently for it until it receives the early and latter rain." – Jas 5:7

In waiting for the Holy Spirit
"And being assembled together with them, He commanded them not to depart from Jerusalem, but to wait for the promise of the Father, which, He said, 'You have heard of me.' " – Acts 1:4

Peace

Should be sought
"Let the peace of God rule in your hearts, to which also you were called in one body; and be thankful." – Col 3:15

Should be given by Jesus
"These things I have spoken to you, that in Me you may have peace." – John 16:33

Should pass understanding,
"The peace of God, which surpasses all understanding, will guard your hearts and minds through Christ Jesus." – Phil 4:7

Should follow peace and holiness
"Pursue peace with all men, and holiness, without which no one will see the Lord." – Heb 12:14

Perseverance

In well-doing
"Let us not grow weary while doing good, but in due season we shall reap if we do not lose heart." – Gal 6:9

In Christian living
"We also, since we are surrounded by so great a cloud of witnesses, let us lay aside every weight, and the sin which so easily ensnares us, and let us run with endurance the race that is set before us." – Heb 12:1

Be true to the end
"Gird up the loins on your mind, be sober, and rest your hope fully upon the grace that is to be brought to you at the revelation of Jesus Christ." – I Pet 1:13

Praise

To God in song
"Sing praises to the Lord, who dwells in Zion." – Psa 9:11

With musical instruments
"Praise the Lord with the harp: make melody to Him with an instrument of ten strings." – Psa 33:2

With universal praise given to God
"Let the people praise You, O God: let all the people praise You." – Psa 67:3

To God perpetually
"By Him let us continually offer the sacrifice of praise to God, that is, the fruit of our lips, giving thanks to His name." – Heb 13:15

For four reasons
"You are a chosen generation, a royal priesthood, a holy nation, His own special people, that you may proclaim the graces of Him who called you out of darkness into His marvelous light." – I Pet 2:9

Rejoicing

Because our names are written in heaven
"Do not rejoice in this, that the spirits are subject to you, but rather rejoice because your names are written in heaven." – Lk 10:20

With fellowmen
"Rejoice with those who rejoice, and weep with those who weep." – Rom 12:15

In the Lord always
"Rejoice in the Lord always. Again I will say, 'Rejoice.'" – Phil 4:4

To be a part of Christ's suffering
"Rejoice to the extent that you partake of Christ's sufferings, that when His glory is revealed, you may also be glad with exceeding joy." - I Pet 4:13

At answered prayer
"Until now you have asked nothing in my name. Ask and you will receive that your joy may be full." – John 16:24

Renunciation

Willing to leave home and friends
"See we have left all and followed you." – Mk 10:28

Willing to leave a business
"He left all, rose up, and followed Him. Then Levi gave Him a great feast in his own house." – Luke 5:28, 29

Forsaking all to follow Christ
"So likewise, whoever of you does not forsake all that he has cannot be my disciple." – Lk 14:33

Will be rewarded
"He said to them, 'Assuredly, I say to you, there is no one who has left house or parents or brothers or wife or children, for the sake of the kingdom of God, who shall not receive many times more in this present time, and in the age to come.' " – Lk 18:29, 30

Respect

Children for parents
"For God commanded, saying, 'Honor your father and your mother.' " – Matt 15:4

Youth for elders
"Do not rebuke an older man, but exhort him as a father, the younger men as brothers." – I Tim 5:1

Given to Christ
"Let us be glad and rejoice and give him glory." – Rev 19:7

Given to God and all men
"Honor all people. Love the brotherhood. Fear God. Honor the king." – I Pet 2:17

Responsibility

For our words
"I say unto you that for every idle word men may speak, they will give account of it in the day of judgment." – Matt 12:36

For our money
"So it was that when he returned, having received the kingdom, he then commanded these servants, to whom he has given the money, to be called to him, that he might know how much every man had gained by trading." – Lk 19:15

For our lives
"So each of us shall give account of himself to God." – Rom 14:12

Reverence

For God
"Let all the earth fear the Lord." – Psa 33:8

For the sanctuary
"And He said to those who sold doves, 'Take these things away: Do not make my Father's house a house of merchandise.' " – John 2:16

For God's name
"In this manner, therefore, pray. 'Our Father in heaven, hallowed be thy name.' " – Matt 6:9

For men of God
"We urge you, brethren, to recognize those who labor among you, and are over you in the Lord and admonish you, and to esteem them very highly in love for their works sake." – I Thess 5:12, 13

For parents
"God commanded, saying, "Honor your father and your mother." – Matt 15:4

For religious leaders
"Remember those who rule over you, who have spoken the Word of God to you, whose faith follow, considering the outcome of their conduct." – Heb 13:7

For the Word of God
"If anyone takes away from the words of the book of this prophecy, God shall take away his part from the Book of Life, from the Holy City, and from the things which are written in this book." – Rev 22:19

Soberness

To be watchful
"Let us not sleep, as others do, but let us watch and be sober." – I Thess 5:6

The teaching of God's grace
"For the grace of God that brings salvation has appeared to all men, teaching us, that denying ungodliness and worldly lusts, we should live soberly, righteously and godly in the present age." – Titus 2:11, 12

To be ready for the end time
"The end of all things is at hand; therefore be serious and watchful in your prayers." – I Pet 4:7

Solicitude

"Out of much affliction and anguish of heart I wrote to you, with many tears, not that you should be grieved, but that you might know the love which I have so abundantly for you." - II Cor 2:4

Sympathy

For those who need help
"Then they all wept freely, and fell on Paul's neck and kissed him, sorrowing most of all for the words which he spoke, that they would see his face no more." – Acts 20:37, 38

For the weak
"We then who are strong ought to bear with the scruples of the weak, and not to please ourselves." – Rom 15:1

For the unfortunate
"Remember the prisoners as if chained with them, and those who are mistreated, since you yourselves are in the body also." – Heb 13:3
For widows
"Pure and undefiled religion before God and the Father is this: to visit orphans and widows in their trouble, and to keep oneself unspotted from the world." – Jas 1:27
Bear one another's burdens
"Bear one another's burdens, and so fulfill the law of Christ." – Gal 6:22

Thankfulness

For our spiritual inheritance
"…giving thanks to the Father who has qualified us to be partakers of the inheritance of the saints in the light." – Col 1:12
For God's peace
"Let the peace of God rule in your hearts…and be thankful." – Col 3:15
For everything
"In everything give thanks; for this is the will of God." – I Thess 5:18

Tolerance

For other religions
"Teacher, we saw someone who does not follow us…do not forbid him…for he who is not against us is on our side." – Mark 9:38-41
For other servants of God
Mark 9:38-39 (same as above)

Trust

Trust God to guide
"Commit your way to the Lord, trust also in Him, and He shall bring it to pass." – Psa 37:5
By commitment to God
"Let those who suffer according to the will of God commit their souls to Him in doing good, as to a faithful Creator." – I Pet 4:19
Trust with a whole heart
"Trust in the Lord with all your heart and lean not on your own understanding.' – Prov 3:5
No need to worry
"Let not your heart be troubled; ye believe in God, believe also in me." – John 14:1
Read Matthew 6:25-32

Watchfulness

For the coming of Christ
"Watch therefore, for you know neither the day nor the hour in which the son of Man cometh." – Matt 25:13

God's children do not sleep
"You are all sons of light and sons of the day. We are not of the night nor of darkness. Therefore let us not sleep, as others do, but let us watch and be sober." – I Thess 5:5, 6

Against sin and temptation
"Watch and pray lest ye enter into temptation." – Matt 26:41

Against falling
"Let him who thinks he stands take heed lest he fall." – I Cor 10:12

To be faithful
"Watch, stand fast in the faith, be brave, be strong." – I Cor 16:13

In prayer
"Continue earnestly in prayer, being vigilant in it with thanksgiving." – Col 4:2

Against the devil
"Be sober, be vigilant, because your adversary the devil walks about like a roaring lion, seeking whom he may devour." – I Pet 5:8

For the coming of Christ
Read Mark 13:32-37

For false prophets
Matt 7:15-20

Our character at the end time
"Since all things will be dissolved, what manner of person ought you to be in holy conduct and godliness." – II Pet 3:11

Against backsliding
Read Heb 3:12

Spiritual Development

Spiritual Necessities

Conversion
Essential to enter the Kingdom
"Assuredly, unless you are converted and become as little children, you will by no means enter the kingdom of heaven." – Matt 18:3
Preparation for Christian service
"I have prayed for you, that your faith should not fail: and when you have returned to me, strengthen your brethren." – Lk 22:32
The supreme task of the church
"Brethren, if anyone among you wanders from the truth, and someone turns him back, let him know that he who turns a sinner from the error of his way will save a soul from death and cover a multitude of sins." – Jas 5:19, 20

Repentance
Required of all
"Truly these times of ignorance God overlooked, but now commands all men everywhere to repent." – Acts 17:30

Will perish without it
> "I tell you, no, but unless you repent you will all likewise perish." – Lk 13:3

The new birth
> "Jesus answered and said to him, 'Most assuredly, I say to you, unless one is born again, he cannot see the kingdom of God.' " – John 3:5

Inward righteousness
> "For I say to you, that unless your righteousness exceeds the righteousness of the scribes and Pharisees, you will by no means enter the kingdom of heaven." – Matt 5:20

Spiritual worship
> "God is a Spirit, and those who worship him must worship in spirit and truth." – John 4:24

Spiritual food
> "Then Jesus said to them, 'Most assuredly, I say unto you, unless you eat the flesh of the Son of Man and drink His blood, you have no life in you.' " – John 6:53

Personal faith
> "I said to you that you will die in your sins; for if you do not believe that I am He, you will die in your sins." – John 8:24

Sanctification
> "If anyone cleanses himself from the latter, he will be a vessel for honor, sanctified and useful for the Master, prepared for every good work." – II Tim 2:21

Spiritual Characteristics

Abiding

To be close to Christ
> "Abide in me and I in you." – John 15:4-10

To walk like Christ
> "He who says he abides in him ought himself also to walk just as he walked." - I John 2:6

To be ready for the coming of Christ
> "And now, little children, abide in Him, that when He appears, we may have confidence and not be ashamed before Him at His coming." – I John 2:28

To avoid sinning
> "Whoever abides in Him does not sin." – I John 3:6

Chastisement

A mark of God's love
> "For whom the Lord loves He chastens, and scourges every son whom He receives, for if ye endure chastening, God deals with you as with sons, for what son is there whom a father does not chastise?" – Heb 12:6, 7

Path to fruit-bearing
> "Every branch in Me that does not bear fruit He takes away; and every branch that bears fruit He prunes, that it may bear more fruit." – John 15:2

Church attendance
- Not to be forsaken
  - "Not forsaking the assembling of ourselves together." – Heb 10:25
- Follow example of disciples
  - "So continuing daily with one accord in the temple, and breaking bread from house to house." – Acts 2:46, 47

Composure
- In times of war
  - "You will hear of wars and rumors of wars. See that ye are not troubled, for all these things must come to pass, but the end is not yet." – Matt 24:6
- No need for troubled hearts
  - "Let not your heart be troubled; you believe in God, believe also in me." – John 14:1
- Because Jesus is coming again
  - "To give you who are troubled rest with us when the Lord Jesus is revealed from heaven with His mighty angels." – II Thess 1:7
- In times of suffering
  - "For the eyes of the Lord are on the righteous…and who is he who will harm you, if you become followers of what is good? But even if you should suffer for righteousness sake, you are blessed. And do not be afraid of their threats, nor be troubled." – I Pet 3:12-14

Confession of sin
- Leads to God's mercy
  - "He who covers his sins shall not prosper, but whoever confesses and forsakes them shall have mercy." – Prov 28:12
- Leads to forgiveness
  - "If we confess our sins, He is faithful and just to forgive." – I John 1:9

Discernment
- A mark of spiritual maturity
  - "Solid food belongs to those who are of full age, that is, those who by reason of use have their senses exercised to discern both good and evil." – Heb 5:14
- The Lord's gift
  - "Consider what I say, and may the Lord give you understanding in all things." – II Tim 2:7

Food
- Partake of the Living Bread
  - "I am the Living Bread which came down from heaven. If anyone eats of this bread, he will live forever, and the bread that I shall give is my flesh, which I shall give for the life of the world." – John 6:51
- To overcome
  - "To him that overcomes I will give to eat of the tree of life." – Rev 2:7

Forsake sin
- Put off the old man
  - "Put off concerning your former conduct, the old man which grows corrupt." – Eph 4:22
- Lay aside every sin
  - "Since we are surrounded by so great a cloud of witnesses, let us lay aside every weight and the sin which so easily ensnares us, and let us run with endurance the race that is set before us." – Heb 12:1

Fruit
- Must be receptive
  - "He who received seed on the good ground is he who hears the Word and understands it, who indeed bears fruit and produces: some a hundredfold, some sixty, some thirty." – Matt 13:23
- Requires abiding in Christ
  - "I am the vine, you are the branches. He who abides in Me, and I in him, bears much fruit, for without Me ye can do nothing." – John 15:5

Godliness
- Is profitable
  - "Bodily exercise profits a little, but godliness is profitable for all things." – I Tim 4:8
- Should issue in good works
  - "Those who have believed in God should be careful to maintain good works. These are good and profitable to men." – Tit 3:8

Growth
- In fruitfulness
  - "May He who supplies seed to the sower, and bread for food, supply and multiply the seed you have sown and increase the fruits of your righteousness." – II Cor 9:10
- Into Christ
  - "Speaking the truth in love…grow up in all things into Him who is the head – Christ." – Eph 4:15
- In love
  - "May the Lord make you increase and abound in love to one another." – I Thess 3:12
- Unto perfection
  - "Leaving the discussion of the elementary principles in Christ, let us go on to perfection." – Heb 6:1
- Through the Word
  - "As newborn babes, desire the pure milk of the Word, that you may grow thereby." – I Pet 2:2
- In grace and knowledge
  - "Grow in grace and knowledge of our Lord and Savior Jesus Christ." – II Pet 3:18
- Read II Pet 1:5-10

Holiness
- Serve in holiness
    - "Grant us, that we, being delivered from the hand of our enemies, might serve Him without fear, in holiness and righteousness before Him all the days of our lives." – Luke 1:74, 75
- Strive for cleanness
    - "Having these promises dearly beloved, let us cleanse ourselves from all filthiness of the flesh, perfecting holiness in the fear of God." – II Cor 7:1
- Follow it
    - "Pursue peace with all men, and holiness, without which no man will see the Lord." – Heb 12:14
- Be holy because God is holy
    - "It is written, 'Be holy for I am holy.' " – I Pet 1:16

Knowledge
- Spiritual knowledge should be sought
    - "Add to your faith virtue, to virtue, knowledge." – II Pet 1:5
- Liberates the soul
    - "You shall know the truth and the truth shall make you free." – John 8:32
- Leads to eternal life
    - "This is eternal life, that they may know You, the only true God." – John 17:3
- Grows in grace
    - "Grow in grace and knowledge of our Lord and Savior Jesus Christ." – II Pet 3:18

Maturity
- Put away childish things
    - "When I became a man, I put away childish things." – I Cor 13:11
- Cultivate understanding
    - "Do not be children in understanding…be mature." – I Cor 14:20
- Strive for the ideal of Christ
    - "Till we all come to the unity of the faith…to the measure of the stature of the fullness of Christ." – Eph 4:13
- Partake of the deeper truth of the Gospel
    - "Solid food belongs to those who are of full age." – Heb 5:14
- Achieve by overcoming temptation
    - "I have written to you…because you are strong…you have overcome the wicked one." – I John 2:14

Meditation
- On the things of God
    - "Meditate on these things…that your progress may be evident to all." – I Tim 4:15
- On the law
    - "His delight is in the law of the Lord." – Psa 1:2

Mind
    Cultivate a spiritual mind
        "To be carnally minded is death, but to be spiritual minded is life and peace." – Rom 8:6
    Cultivate the mind of Christ
        "Let this mind be in you, which was also in Christ Jesus." – Phil 2:5
    Think wise thoughts
        "Brethren, whatsoever things are true, whatsoever things are noble, whatsoever things are just, whatsoever things are pure, whatever things are lovely, whatsoever things are of good report --- meditate on these things." – Phil 4:8
    Prove what is good
        "Test all things; hold fast what is good." – I Thess 5:21
    Try the spirits
        "Do not believe every spirit, but test the spirits, whether they are of God; because many false prophets have gone out into the world." – I John 4:1
    Mold all thoughts captive to Christ
        "Bringing every thought into captivity to the obedience of Christ." – II Cor 10:5
    Ask for wisdom
        "If any of you lack wisdom, let him ask of God who gives to all liberally and without reproach, and it will be given him." – Jas 1:5

Perfection
    Emulate God
        "You shall be perfect, just as your Father in heaven is perfect." – Matt 5:48
    Strive for it
        "We all (should) come to the unity of the faith and the knowledge of the Son of God, to a perfect man, to the measure of the stature of the fullness of Christ." – Eph 4:13
    Go on beyond the foundations
        "Leaving the discussion of the elementary principles of Christ, let us go on to perfection." – Heb 6:1

Quietness
    Study to be quiet as we live
        "Aspire to lead a quiet life, to mind your own business." – I Thess 4:11
    Exhibit gentleness
        "Let it be the hidden person of the heart, with the incorruptible ornament of a gentle and quiet spirit, which is very precious in the sight of the Lord." – I Pet 3:4
    Know God
        "Be still and know that I am God." – Psa 46:10a

Resistance to the Devil
    Withstand the devil
        (Do not) "give place to the Devil." – Eph 4:27

Put on the whole armor of God
> "Put on the whole armor of God, that ye may be able to stand against the wiles of the Devil." – Eph 6:11

Be watchful
> "Be sober, be vigilant, because your adversary the Devil walks about like a roaring lion." – I Pet 5:8

Resistance of temptation

To receive the victory
> "Blessed is the man who endures temptation; for when he has been proved, he will receive the crown of life." – Jas 1:12

To misuse our members
> "Do not present your members as instruments of unrighteousness to sin, but present yourselves to God as being alive from the dead, and your members as instruments of righteousness to God." – Rom 6:13

Restraint of appetites

By subduing fleshly lusts
> "Put on the Lord Jesus Christ, and make no provision for the flesh, to fulfill its lusts." – Rom 13:14

By walking in the Spirit
> "Walk in the Spirit, and you shall not fulfill the lust of the flesh." – Gal 5:16

By mortifying our members
> "Put to death your members which are on the earth: fornication, uncleanness, passion, evil desire, and covetousness." – Col 3:5

By devaluation of things
> "Do not worry about your life, what you will eat; nor about the body, what you will wear." – Lk 12:22

By keeping the body under subjection
> "I discipline my body and bring it into subjection, lest, when I have preached to others, I myself should become disqualified." – I Cor 9:27

By rejecting the world
> "Do not love the world of the things in the world." – I John 2:15-17

Righteousness

Exceeding formal religion
> "Unless your righteousness exceeds the righteousness of the scribes and Pharisees, you will by no means enter the kingdom of heaven." – Matt 5:20

Manifesting the fruits of righteousness
> "Being filled with the fruits of righteousness which are by Jesus Christ." – Phil 1:11

Search the Word

Because it speaks of Jesus
> "You search the Scriptures, for in them you think you have eternal life; and these are they which testify of Me." – John 5:39

Because it teaches us
    "Whatever things were written before were written for our learning." – Rom 15:4
Because it provides wisdom
    "Let the word of Christ dwell in you richly in all wisdom." – Col 3:16
Because it results in spiritual growth
    "Desire the pure milk of the word that you may grow thereby." - I Pet 2:2

Search for gifts
    To discover and use our talents
        "He who had received five talents came and brought five other talents." – Matt 25:20
    Desire spiritual gifts
        "Pursue love, and desire spiritual gifts…that you may prophesy." – I Cor 14:1
    Covet the best gifts
        "Earnestly desire the best gifts." – I Cor 12:31

Self-control
    Over one's spirit
        "Understanding is a well-spring of life to him who has it, but correction of fools is folly." – Prov 16:22
    Over the life
        "Now as he reasoned about righteousness and self-control, and the judgment to come, Felix was afraid and answered, 'Go away for now; when I have a convenient time I will call for you.' " – Acts 24:25
    Over the lusts of the flesh
        "Do not let sin reign in your mortal body, so that you should obey it in its lusts." – Rom 6:12
    Over the tongue
        "If anyone does not stumble in word, he is a perfect man, also able to bridle the whole body." – Jas 3:2
    A cardinal virtue
        "Giving all diligence, add to your faith virtue." – II Pet 1:5
    Over the body
        "I discipline my body and bring it into subjection." – I Cor 9:27

Self-denial
    To take up the cross
        "If anyone desires to come after Me, let him deny himself, and take up his cross and follow Me." – Matt 16:24
    To crucify the flesh
        "Those who are Christ's have crucified the flesh with its passions and desires." – Gal 5:24
    To follow Jesus
        "If anyone desires to come after Me, let him deny himself, and take up his cross and follow Me." – Lk 9:23

Self-examination
- To prove selves
  - "Examine yourselves as to whether you are in the faith. Prove yourselves." – II Cor 13:5
- To prove our own work
  - "Let him who is taught the word share in all good things with him who teaches…but let each one examine his own work." – Gal 6:6, 4

Self-sacrifice
- To save our lives
  - "Whoever desires to save his life will lose it, and whoever loses his life for My sake will find it." – Matt 16:36
- To avoid offending others
  - "It is good neither to eat meat nor drink wine nor do anything by which your brother stumbles or is offended or is made weak." – Rom 14:21
- To put others ahead of self
  - "Let no one seek his own, but each one the other's well being." – I Cor 10:24

Surrendered life
- Means death to sin
  - "Reckon yourselves to be dead indeed to sin, but alive to God in Jesus Christ our Lord." – Rom 6:11
- Means completely yielded to God
  - "Do not present your members as instruments of unrighteousness to sin but present yourselves to God as being alive from the dead, and your members as instruments of righteousness to God." – Rom 6:13
- Means hidden with Christ
  - "Set your mind on things which are above, not on things on this earth, for you died, and your life is hidden with Christ in God." – Col. 3:2, 3
- Means complete consecration
  - "I beseech you brethren, by the mercies of God, that you present your bodies a living sacrifice, holy, acceptable to God, which is your reasonable service." – Rom 12:1, 2

THE BELIEVER'S WALK

The Nature of This Walk

A walk before God
"Brethren, we urge and exhort in the Lord Jesus that you should abound more and more, just as you received from us how you ought to walk and to please God." – I Thess 4:1

A walk with God
"Enoch walked with God, and he was not, for God took him." – Gen 5:24

A walk of faith
"We walk by faith, not by sight." – II Cor 5:7

The Characteristics of This Walk

Spirituality
"Walk in the Spirit, and you shall not fulfill the lusts of the flesh." – Gal 5:16

Consistency
"I…beseech you to walk worthy of the calling with which you were called." – Eph 4:1

Caution
"See then that you walk circumspectly, not as fools but as wise." – Eph 5:15

Illumination
"If we walk in the light as He is in the light, we have fellowship with one another, and the blood of Jesus Christ His son cleanses us from all sin." – I John 1:7

Christlikeness
"He who says he abides in Him ought himself also to walk just as He walked." – I John 2:6

The Practice of This Walk

Walk circumspectly
"See then that you walk circumspectly, not as fools but as wise." – Eph 5:15

Walk in the light
"If we walk in the light as He is in the light, we have fellowship with one another, and the blood of Jesus Christ cleanses us from all sin." – I John 1:7

Walk cheerfully
"Do not be drunk with wine…but be filled with the Spirit." – Eph 5:18

Walk in love
"Walk in love, as Christ also has loved us." – Eph 5:2

Walk in newness of life
"Just as Christ was raised from the dead by the glory of the Father, even so we also should walk in newness of life." – Rom 6:4

Walk in truth
"Teach me your way, O Lord: I will walk in your truth." – Psa 86:11

Walk in wisdom
"Walk in wisdom toward those who are outside, redeeming the time." – Col 4:5

Walk worthily
> "I beseech you…to walk worthy of the calling with which you were called." – Eph 4:1

SACRED AND RELIGIOUS RESPONSIBILITIES

Introduction

Sacred and religious duties are given specific attention in the Scripture. There are personal responsibilities each professing Christian should seek to develop. These include such matters as faith, fasting, giving, observing the Lord's supper, prayer life, service, stewardship, witnessing, and worship.

Ministerial responsibilities are carefully dealt with. These are duties which are due to ministers, as well as the duties of ministers.

Duties of the church in its responsibility to support the ministry are given. Not to be overlooked is the part played by women in ministry.

PERSONAL RESPONSIBILITIES

Faith

A fundamental duty
> "They said to Him, 'What shall we do, that we may work the works of God?' Jesus answered and said to them, 'This is the work of God, that you believe in Him whom He sent.'" – John 6:28, 29

An indispensable element in religion
> "Without faith it is impossible to please Him, for he who comes to God must believe that He is." – Heb 11:6

Justified by faith
> "Having been justified by faith, we have peace with God." – Rom 5:1

Secures salvation
> "Most assuredly, I say to you, he who hears my word and believes in Him who sent me has everlasting life, and shall not come into judgment, but has passed from death into life." - John 5:24
>
> "If you confess with your mouth the Lord Jesus and believe in your heart that God raised Him from the dead, you will be saved." Rom 10:9

We stand by faith
> "By faith you stand." – II Cor 1:24

Issue in eternal life
> "This is the will of Him Who sent Me, that everyone who sees the Son and believes in Him may have everlasting life." – John 6:40

A defensive weapon
"Take the shield of faith with which you will be able to quench all the fiery darts of the wicked one." – Eph 6:16

Read John 3:14-16

Essential in prayer life
"If any of you lack wisdom, let him ask of God, who gives to all liberally and without reproach, and it will be given you. But let him ask in faith, with no doubting." – Jas 1:5, 6

Should be united with love
"This is His commandment: that we should believe on the name of His Son Jesus Christ and love one another, as He gave us commandment." – I John 3:23

Fasting

To please God
"You, when you fast, anoint your head and wash your face, so that you do not appear to men to be fasting, but to your Father who is in the secret place, and your Father who sees in secret will reward you openly." – Matt 6:17, 18

To make prayer effective
(about casting out demons) "This kind does not go out except by prayer and fasting." – Matt 17:21

To follow the example of Jesus
"Then, Jesus, being filled with the Holy Spirit, returned from the Jordan, and was led by the Spirit into the wilderness, being tempted for forty days by the devil. And in those days He ate nothing."
– Lk 4:1, 2

Giving

Honor God
"Honor the Lord with your possession, and with the first fruits of your increase." – Prov 3:9

Do without ostentation
"When you do a charitable deed, do not let your left hand know what your right hand is doing." – Matt 6:3

Give freely
"Freely you have received, freely give." – Matt 10:8

Give with simplicity
"He who gives, with liberality." – Rom 12:8

Give regularly
"On the first day of the week let each one of you lay something aside, storing up as he may prosper." – I Cor 16:2

Give cheerfully
"Let each one give as he purposes in his heart, not grudgingly or of necessity, for God loves a cheerful giver." – II Cor 9:7

Give tithes
"Bring all the tithes into the storehouse." – Mal 3:10

Give alms
"Give alms of such things as you have." – Lk 11:41

Give liberally
"Give, and it will be given you, good measure, pressed down." – Lk 6:38

It is blessed
"It is more blessed to give than to receive." – Acts 20:35

Prayer

We are to pray to overcome temptation
"Watch and pray, lest you enter into temptation." – Matt 26:41

We are free to ask in prayer
"Ask, and you will receive, that your joy may be full." – John 16:24

We are to pray in the Spirit
"Praying always with all prayer and supplication in the Spirit." – Eph 6:18

We are to pray without ceasing
"Pray without ceasing." – I Thess 5:17

We are to pray for the sick
"Is anyone among you suffering? Let him pray...is anyone among you sick? Let him call for the elders of the church, and let them pray over him." – Jas 5:13, 14

We are to pray in communion with others
"I say to you that if two of you agree on earth as concerning anything that they ask, it will be done for them by my Father in heaven." – Matt 18:19

We are to pray by faith
"I say to you, whatever things you ask when you pray, believe that you receive them and you will have them." – Mk 11:24

We are to pray in secret
"When you pray, go into your room, and when you have shut your door, pray to your Father, Who is in the secret place, and your Father who seeks in secret will reward you openly." – Matt 6:6

We are to ask, seek, and knock
    "Ask and it will be given to you, seek, and you will find; knock and it will be opened to you." – Matt 7:7

We are to pray for food
    "Give us this day our daily bread." – Matt 6:11

We are to pray for our enemies
    "Pray for those who spitefully use you and persecute you." – Matt 5:44

We are to avoid vain repetitions
    "When you pray, you shall not be like the hypocrites…for they pray that they may be seen of men." – Matt 6:7

We are to pray for people to serve
    "Pray the Lord of the harvest to send out laborers into His harvest." – Matt 9:38

We are to use the Lord's Prayer as a model.
    Read Matt 11:2-4.

We are to answer prayers of those in need
    "Give to him who asks you and to him who wants to borrow from you, turn not away." – Matt 5:42

We are to pray with thanksgiving
    "Continue earnestly in prayer, being vigilant in it with thanksgiving." – Col 4:2

We are to pray for healing
    "Confess your trespasses to one another, and pray for one another, that you may be healed." – Jas 5:16

We are to pray in Jesus' name
    "Whatever you ask in my name, that I will do." – John 14:13

We are to pray for wisdom
    "If any of you lacks wisdom, let him ask of God." – Jas 1:5

Service

It ennobles life
    "Whoever desires to become great among you, shall be your servant. And whoever of you desires to be first shall be last of all." – Mk 10:43, 44

It is Christlike
    "Whatever you ask in my name, that I will do, that the Father may be glorified in the Son." - John 14:13
    "If I then, your Lord and Teacher have washed your feet, you also ought to wash one another's feet!" - John 13:14

It demonstrates love
"He said to them a second time, 'Simon, son of Jonah, do you love Me?' He said to him, 'Yes, Lord, you know that I love you.' He said to him, 'Tend my sheep!' " – John 21:16

It lightens life's burdens
"Bear one another's burdens, and so fulfill the law of Christ...As we have opportunity, let us do good to all, especially to those who are of the household of faith." – Gal 6:2, 10

It should be performed in humility
"Serving the Lord with all humility." – Acts 20:19

It should be done in purity
"If anyone cleanses himself from the latter, he will be a vessel for honor, sanctified, and useful for the Master." – II Tim 2:21

We should be ready for every good work
"Remind them to be subject to rulers and authorities, to obey, to be ready for every good work." – Tit 3:1

Our service for Christ is an honor
"If anyone serves Me, him will my Father honor." – John 12:26

Service will result in reward
"Whatever you do, do it heartily, as to the Lord and not to men, knowing that from the Lord you will receive the reward of the inheritance; for you serve the Lord Christ." – Col 3:23, 24

Service glorifies God
"Let your light so shine before men, that they may see your good works and glorify your Father in heaven." – Matt 5:16

Service enriches life
"Let them do good, that they may be rich in good works, ready to give, willing to share." – I Tim 6:18

Service provides a good example
"In all things showing yourself a pattern of good works." – Tit 2:7

Service motivates others to do so
"Let us consider one another in order to stir up love and good works." – Heb 10:24

Service demonstrates the reality of our faith
"Someone will say, 'You have faith and I have works.' Show me your faith without your works, and I will show you my faith by my works." – Jas 2:18

Service is commanded
"Do not forget to do good and to share, for with such sacrifices God is well pleased." – Heb 13:16

Service helps to save souls
"Let him know that he who turns a sinner from the error of his way will save a soul from death and cover a multitude of sins." – Jas 5:20

Service leads to greatness
"Whoever desires to be great among you, let him be your servant." – Matt 20:26

Service is based on the Great Commission
"Jesus spoke to them, saying, 'All authority has been given to Me in heaven and in earth. Go, therefore, and make disciples of all the nations.' " – Matt 28:18-20

Service means to do good for all men
"As we have opportunity, let us do good to all." – Gal 6:10

Service means not to be weary in well-doing
"Do not grow weary in doing good." – II Thess 3:13

Read Matt 25:31-46; Lk 19:11-26.

Stewardship

It means the use of our talents
"The kingdom of heaven is like a man traveling to a far country, who called his own servants and delivered his goods to them. And to one he gave five talents, to another two, and to another one, to each according to his own ability, and immediately he went on a journey." – Matt 25:14, 15

It means to be faithful
"It is required in stewards that one be found faithful." – I Cor 4:2

It means that life is precious
"You were bought at a price, therefore glorify God in your body and in your spirit, which are God's." – I Cor 6:20

It means to minister
"As each one has received a gift, minister it to one another, as good stewards of the manifold grace of God." – I Pet 4:10

It means to be accountable
"Each of us shall give account of himself to God." – Rom 14:12

It means the right use of possessions
"Seek first the kingdom of God and His righteousness and all these things shall be added to you." – Matt 6:33

It means the right use of money
(See Giving above).

Witnessing

It means to bear witness
"You also shall bear witness, because you have been with Me from the beginning." – John 15:27

It means to let our lights shine
"Let your light so shine before men, that they may see your good works and glorify your Father in heaven." – Matt 5:16

It means to confess Christ
"Whoever shall confess Me before men, him will I also confess before My Father who is in heaven." – Matt 10:32

It means to witness in the power of the Holy Spirit
"You shall receive power when the Holy Spirit has come upon you, and you shall be witnesses to Me." – Acts 1:8

It leads to salvation
"If you confess with your mouth the Lord Jesus and believe in your heart that God has raised Him from the dead, you will be saved." – Rom 10:9, 10

As chosen people we are to praise Him
"You are a chosen generation, a royal priesthood, a holy nation, His own special people that you may proclaim the praises of Him Who called you out of darkness into His marvelous light." – I Pet 2:9

Worship (See Duties to Deity)

MINISTERIAL RESPONSIBILITIES

Duties to Ministers

Honor them as servants of Christ
"We do not preach ourselves, but Christ Jesus the Lord, and ourselves your servants for Jesus' sake." – II Cor 4:5

Honor them because they have faith and preach the Word
"Remember those who rule over you, who have spoken the Word of God to you, whose faith follow, considering the outcome of their conduct." – Heb 13:7

Duties of Ministers

General Responsibilities
To administer
"For this reason I left you in Crete, that you should set in order the things that are lacking and appoint elders in every city as I commanded you." – Tit 1:5

To divinely appoint
"(Christ) who made us sufficient as ministers of the new covenant, not of the letter of the Spirit, for the letter kills, but the Spirit gives life." - II Cor 3:6
"God…has given us the ministry of reconciliation." - II Cor 5:18
"I thank Christ Jesus our Lord, Who has enabled me, because He counted me faithful, putting me into the ministry." - I Tim 1:12

To carry out the Great Commission
"Go, therefore, and make disciples of all nations." – Matt 28:19

To pray and study the Word
"We will give ourselves continually to prayer and to the ministry of the Word." – Acts 6:4

To provide a good example
"In all things showing yourselves to be a pattern of good works, in doctrine showing integrity, reverence, incorruptibility, sound speech, that cannot be condemned, that one who is an opponent may be ashamed, having nothing evil to say of you." – Tit 2:7, 8

To follow and fight
Read I Tim 6:1-12

To find and use gifts
Read I Cor 12:28-31
Read I Tim 4:6-16; Chapter 5

To preach
Preach the Word
"Preach the Word. Be ready in season and out of season. Convince, rebuke, exhort, with all longsuffering and teaching." – II Tim 4:2

Preach the Kingdom of Heaven
"And, as you go, preach, saying, 'The kingdom of heaven is at hand.' " – Matt 10:7

Preach to all the world
"Go into all the world and preach the gospel to every creature." – Mk 16:15

Preach and heal
"He sent them to preach the kingdom of God and to heal the sick." – Lk 9:2

Preach the words of life
"Go, stand in the temple and speak to the people all the words of this life." – Acts 5:20

Preaching a divine obligation
"If I preach the gospel, I have nothing to boast of, for necessity is laid upon me, yea, woe is me if I do not preach the gospel." – I Cor 9:16

Preach Christ
Preach Christ crucified
"We preach Christ crucified, to the Jews a stumbling block and to the Greeks foolishness." – I Cor 1:23

Preach Christ as Lord
"For we do not preach ourselves, but Christ Jesus the Lord." – II Cor 4:5

Preach simply
- Be humble
    - "And I, brethren, when I came to you, did not come with excellence of speech or of wisdom declaring to you the testimony of God." – I Cor 2:1
- Adapt to needs of hearers
    - "I fed you with milk and not with solid food; for until now you were not able to receive it." – I Cor 3:2
- Be gentle
    - "A servant of the Lord must not quarrel, but be gentle to all, able to teach, patient." – II Tim 2:24

Teach
- By observation of all that Jesus taught
    - "Teaching them to observe all things that I have commanded you." – Matt 28:20
- By command
    - "These things command and teach." – I Tim 4:11
- By means of instruction
    - "(Teach) in humility correcting those who are in opposition." – II Tim 2:25

Feed the flock (shepherd)
- To please the Lord "Jesus said to Simon, 'Simon, son of Jonah, do you love me more than these?...Feed My lambs...tend My sheep...feed my sheep.' " – John 21:15-17
- By overseeing "Take heed to yourselves and to all the flock, among which the Holy Spirit has made you overseers." – Acts 20:28

Warn and Admonish
- Warn the unruly
    - "Give no opportunity to the adversary to speak reproachfully." – I Tim 5:14
- Admonish one another
    - "I am confident...that you...are able to admonish one another." – Rom. 15:14
- Teach the Word
    - "Let the Word of Christ dwell in you richly in all wisdom, teaching and admonishing one another." – Col 3:16
- Admonish heretics
    - "Reject a divisive man after the first and second admonition." – Tit 3:10

Watch over Souls
- Ask for obedience
    - "Obey those who rule over you, and be submissive, for they watch over your souls." – Heb 13:17
- Stress life and death
    - "To one we are the aroma of death to death, and to the other the aroma of life to life." – II Cor 2:16

Stewardship
Of the gospel
"For if I do this willingly, I have a reward; but if against my will, I have been entrusted with a stewardship." – I Cor 9:17

Through preaching
"(God) has in due time manifested His Word through preaching, which was committed to me according to the commandment of God our Savior." – Tit 1:3

Duties of Bishops – Read I Tim 3:1-7

Duties of Deacons – Read II Tim 3:8-13

Duties of the Church

Should send preachers
"How shall they preach unless they are sent?" – Rom 10:15

Should pray for workers
"I beg you, brethren, through the Lord Jesus Christ, and through the love of the Spirit, that you strive together with me in your prayers to God for me." – Rom 15:30

Should receive Christian workers
"You received me as an angel of God, even as Christ Jesus." – Gal 4:14

Should esteem Christian workers highly
"(Those over you) esteem them highly in love for their work's sake." – I Thess 5:12, 13

Should follow example of Christian workers
"Remember those who rule over you…considering the outcome of their conduct." – Heb 13:7

Should support Christian workers
"The Lord has commanded that those who preach the gospel should live from the gospel." – I Cor 9:14

Should obey the teachings of Christian workers
"Obey those who rule over you, and be submissive, for they watch for your souls, as those who must give account." – Heb 13:17

Should provide assemblies of worship
"Not forsaking the assembling of ourselves together." – Heb. 10:25

Women's Ministry

They serve the church
"I commend to you Phoebe our sister, who is a servant of the church in Cenchrea, and that you receive her in the Lord in a manner worthy of the saints, and assist her in whatever business she has need of you, for indeed she has been a helper of many and of myself also." – Rom 16:1, 2

They are co-workers with ministers
"Greet Priscilla and Aquila, my fellow workers in Christ Jesus." – Rom 16:3

They help care for ministers
"Greet Mary, who labored much for us." – Rom 16:6

They should perform good works
"Well reported for good works." – I Tim 5:10

SOCIAL DUTIES

Introduction

A great deal of attention in Scripture is given to the social duties of Christians. The Christian faith should be expressed, not only in personal spiritual development, but also in everyday life.

There are individual responsibilities which Christians need to observe in the practices of daily Christian living. Most certainly, the maintenance of a Christian home is a high priority. Duties in this regard involve all family members.

Outside the home in society there are involvements in community life, government, and various relationships with others. Christian men have particular roles to play in relation to home, family and others.

Individual Responsibilities

Almsgiving

Do not give to be noticed
"Take heed that you do not do your charitable deeds before men."
– Matt 6:1

Give to the poor
"If you want to be perfect, go sell what you have and give to the poor."
– Matt 19:21

Must give because we love
"Though I bestow all my goods to feed the poor, and though I give my body to be burned, but have not love, it profits me nothing."
– I Cor 13:3

Benevolence

Be willing to lend
"Give to him who asks you, and from him who wants to borrow from you do not turn away." – Matt 5:42

Give to the weak
"I have shown you in every way, by laboring like this, that you must support the weak. And remember the words of the Lord Jesus, that He said, 'It is more blessed to give than to receive.' " – Acts 20:35

Be generous
"Give, and it will be given to you; good measure, pressed down, shaken together, and running over will be put into your bosom. For with the same measure that you use, it will be measured back to you." – Lk 6:38

Brotherly Love

Should be unselfish
"You shall love your neighbor as yourself." – Matt 22:39

Shows our discipleship
"By this all will know that you are my disciples, if you have love for one another." – John 13:35

Commended by Christ
"This is my commandment, that you love one another, as I have loved you…a new commandment I give to you, that you love one another, as I have loved you, that you also love one another." – John 15:12; 13:34

Should be sincere
"Let love be without hypocrisy." – Rom 12:9

Should abound
"May the Lord make you increase and abound in love to one another and to all, just as we do to you." – I Thess 3:12

Should be fervent
"Love one another fervently with a pure heart." – I Pet 1:22

Shows that we walk in the light
"He who loves his brother abides in the light, and there is no cause for stumbling in him." – I John 2:10

Shows that we have eternal life
"We know that we have passed from death to life, because we love the brethren." - I John 3:14

Shows that we love God
"Beloved, let us love one another, for love is of God: and everyone who loves is born of God and knows God." – I John 4:7

Chastity

Should avoid lust
"I say to you that whoever looks at a woman to lust for her has already committed adultery with her in his heart." – Matt 5:28

Should avoid fornication
"For this is the will of God, your sanctification; that you should abstain from sexual immorality." – I Thess 4:3

Charitableness

Strong should help the weak
"We then who are strong ought to bear the scruples of the weak, and not to please ourselves." – Rom 15:1

Restore those who make mistakes
"Brethren, if a man be overtaken in any trespass, you who are spiritual should restore such a one in the spirit of gentleness, considering yourself lest you also be tempted." – Gal 6:1

Covers a multitude of sins
"Above all things have fervent love for one another, for love will cover a multitude of sins." – I Pet 4:8

Should not judge others
"Judge not that you be not judged, for with what judgment you judge, you will be judged, and with the same measure you use, it will be measured back to you." – Matt 7:1

Civic Righteousness

Exalts a nation
"Righteousness exalts a nation, but sin is a reproach to any people." – Prov 14:34

Results in praiseworthy conduct
"Submit yourselves to every ordinance of man for the Lord's sake, whether to the king as supreme, or to governors, as to those who are sent by him for the punishment of evildoers and for the praise of those who do good." – I Pet 2:13, 14

Compassion

Be like the Good Samaritan
"A certain Samaritan, as he journeyed came where he was. And when he saw him he had compassion on him, and went to him and bandaged his wounds...and took care of him." – Luke 10:33, 34

Should love neighbor as yourself
"You shall love your neighbor as yourself." – Matt 22:39

Consistency

In doctrine and fellowship
"They continued steadfastly in the apostles' doctrine and fellowship." – Acts 2:42

By walking in the light
"If we walk in the light as He is in the light, we have fellowship with one another, and the blood of Jesus Christ His son cleanses us from all sin." – I John 1:7

Courtesy

In our speech
"Let your speech always be with grace, seasoned with salt, that you may know how to answer each one." – Col 4:6

To Christian brethren
"All of you be of one mind, having compassion for one another; love as brothers, be tenderhearted, be courteous." – I Pet 3:8

Fidelity

To be ready for Jesus to come
"Beloved, looking forward to these things (second coming), be diligent to be found by Him in peace, without spot and blameless." – II Pet 3:14

To be a good steward
"It is required in stewards, that one be found faithful." – I Cor 4:2

Good Example

For others to follow
"Make ourselves an example of how you should follow us." – II Thess 3:9

So that it will not offend others
"If food makes my brother stumble, I will never again eat meat, lest I make my brother stumble." – I Cor 8:13

An expression of true love
"He who loves his brother abides in the light, and there is no cause for stumbling in him." – I John 2:10

Judgment

We should not be judgmental
"Jesus said, 'Judge not, that ye be not judged.' " – Matt 7:1

We should not be critical
"Why do you look at the speck in your brother's eye, but do not consider the plank in your own eye?" – Matt 7:3

We should not cast stumbling blocks before other people
Read Romans 14:13

Read Matt 7:1-5

Justice

Render to all their just dues
"Render therefore to all their due: taxes to whom taxes are due; custom to whom customs, fear to whom fear, honor to whom honor." – Rom 13:7

Be just to servants
"Masters give your servants what is just and fair, knowing that you also have a Master in heaven." – Col 4:1

Kindness

A fruit of charity
"Love suffers long and is kind." – I Cor 13:4

Kindness to one another
"Be kind to one another, tenderhearted, forgiving one another, just as God in Christ also forgave you." – Eph 4:32

A cardinal virtue
Read II Peter 1:5-7

The Golden Rule
"Whatever you want men to do to you, do also to them, for this is the law and the prophets." – Matt 7:12

Longsuffering

A fruit of our love
"Love suffers long and is kind." – I Cor 13:4

A fruit of our Christian walk
"Walk worthy…for all patience and longsuffering." – Col 1:10, 11

Compassion based on love
"Be courteous…not returning evil for evil or reviling for reviling, but on the contrary blessings, knowing that you were called to this, that you may inherit a blessing." – I Pet 3:9

Mercifulness

Commanded by Jesus
"Blessed are the merciful, for they shall obtain mercy." – Matt 5:7

Being merciful is God-like
"Be merciful, just as your Father also is merciful." – Lk 6:36

Peaceableness

Live peacefully with all men
"If it is possible, as much as depends on you, live peaceably with all men." – Rom 12:18

Follow peace and holiness
"Pursue peace with all men, and holiness, without which no one will see the Lord." – Heb 12:14

Do all things without duplicity
"Do all things without murmuring and disputing." – Phil 2:14

Peacemakers

All blessed and called children of God
"Blessed are the peacemakers, for they shall be called sons of God." – Matt 5:9

All should seek peace at all times
"Let us pursue the things which make for peace and the things by which one may edify another." – Rom 14:19

Reproof

Rebuke people for trespasses
"Take heed to yourselves. If your brother sins against you, rebuke him, and if he repents, forgive him." – Lk 17:3

Reprove the works of darkness
"Have no fellowship with the unfruitful works of darkness, but rather expose them." – Eph 5:11

Rebuke those who sin
"Those who are sinning rebuke in the presence of all, that the rest also may fear." – I Tim 5:20

Sympathy

For the weak
"You must support the weak." – Acts 20:35

For one another's burden
"Bear one another's burdens, and so fulfill the law of Christ." – Gal 6:2

For those in bonds
"Remember the prisoners as if chained with them, and those who are mistreated." – Heb 13:3

For the needy
"Pure and undefiled religion before God and the Father is this: to visit orphans and widows in their trouble, and to keep oneself unspotted from the world." – Jas 1:27

Temperance

Restrain the appetites
"Take heed to yourselves, lest your hearts be weighed down with carousing, drunkenness, and cares of this life, and that day come on you unexpectedly." – Lk 21:34

Keep the body under
"I discipline my body and bring it into subjection, lest, when I have preached to others, I myself should become disqualified." – I Cor 9:27

Subdue fleshly lusts
"Put on the Lord Jesus Christ, and make no provision for the flesh, to fulfill its lusts." – Rom 13:14

Present yourself to complete consecration
"I beseech you, therefore, brethren, by the mercies of God, that you present your bodies a living sacrifice, holy, acceptable to God, which is your reasonable service." – Rom 12:1

Truthfulness

Speak truth
"Putting away lying, each one speak truth with his neighbor." – Eph 4:25

Do not lie
"Do not lie to one another, since you have put off the old man with his deeds." – Col 3:9

Unity

Strive to keep it
"Endeavoring to keep the unity of the Spirit in the bond of peace." – Eph 4:3

Be of one mind
"All of you be of one mind, having compassion for one another." – I Pet 3:8

Visitation of the Sick

Recommendation of Jesus
"I was sick and you visited me." – Matt 25:36

A subject for prayer
"Is anyone among you sick? Let him call for the elders of the church, and let them pray over him." – Jas 5:14

Home Responsibilities

Purposes

The home is the best place to show piety
"If any widow has children or grandchildren, let them first learn to show piety at home and to repay their parents; for this is good and acceptable before God." – I Tim 5:4

A place to witness
"Go home to your friends and tell them what great things the Lord has done for you, and how He has had compassion on you." – Mk 5:19

Parents' Duties

To teach
"These words…you shall teach…diligently to your children, and shall talk of them when you sit in your house." – Deut 6:7

To train
"Train up a child in the way he should go, and when he is old, he will not depart from it." – Prov 22:6

To provide for children
"The children ought not to lay up for the parents, but the parents for the children." – II Cor 12:14

To nurture
"Fathers, do not provoke your children to wrath, but bring them up in the training and admonition of the Lord." – Eph 6:4

To control
"One who rules his own house well, having his children in submission with all reverence." – I Tim 3:4

To love
"Admonish the young women to love their husbands, to love their children." – Tit 2:4

To correct children
"Do not withhold correction from a child." – Prov 23:13

To provide a good example
"I call to remembrance the genuine faith that is in you, which dwelt first in your grandmother Lois, and your mother Eunice." – II Tim 1:5

To provide good gifts to children
"If you then being evil, know how to give good gifts to your children, how much more will your Father who is in heaven give good things to those who ask Him?" – Matt 7:11

Fathers' Duties

To nurture their children
"Fathers...bring them up in the training and admonition of the Lord." – Eph 6:4

To avoid provoking children
"Fathers, do not provoke your children, lest they become discouraged." – Col 3:21

Husbands

To love their wives
"Husbands ought to love their wives as their own bodies; he who loves his wife loves himself." – Eph 5:28

"Husbands, love your wives and do not be bitter toward them." – Col 3:19

To honor their wives
"Husbands, dwell with them (wives) with understanding, giving honor to the wife, as to the weaker vessel, and as being heirs together of the grace of life, that your prayers be not hindered." – I Pet 3:7

To tend to wives' needs
"Let the husband render to his wife the affection due her, and likewise the wife to her husband." – I Cor 7:3

Wives

Should not leave husbands
"Now as to the married I command, yet not I but the Lord: a wife is not to depart from her husband." – I Cor 7:10

Be submissive to husbands
"Wives, submit to your own husbands, as to the Lord." – Eph 5:22

Be sober and faithful
"Wives must be reverent, not slanderers, temperate; faithful in all things." – I Tim 3:11

Render to husbands due benevolence
"Let the husband render to his wife affection due her, and likewise the wife to her husband." – I Cor 7:3

To live chaste lives
"Wives be submissive to your husbands, that even if some do not obey the word, they without a word, may be won by the conduct of their wives." – I Pet 3:1, 2

To develop the heart, not outward appearance
"Do not let your beauty be that of outward adorning of arranging the hair, of wearing gold, or of putting on fine apparel, but let it be the hidden person of the heart." – I Pet 3:3, 4

Children

Should honor parents
"God commanded, saying, 'Honor your father and your mother.' " – Matt 15:4

Should obey parents
"Children, obey your parents in the Lord, for this is right." – Eph 6:1

Should obey parents to please God
"Children, obey your parents in all things, for this is well pleasing to the Lord." – Col 3:20

Should be allowed knowledge of Jesus
"Jesus said, 'Let the little children come to me, and do not forbid them, for of such is the kingdom of God.' " – Matt 19:14

Marriage and Divorce

Marriage commended
"Marriage is honorable among all, and the bed undefiled." – Heb 13:4

Adultery revealed to be the only basis for divorce
"I say to you that whoever divorces his wife for any reason except sexual immorality causes her to commit adultery; and whoever marries a woman who is divorced commits adultery." – Matt 5:32

Marriages should not be destroyed
Read Matt 19:3-6

Civic Responsibilities

Individual Duties

To keep the law
"Submit yourselves to every ordinance of man for the Lord's sake; whether to the king as supreme, or to governors, as to those who are sent by him for the punishments of evildoers and for the praise of those who do good." – I Pet 2:13, 14

To pay taxes
"Lest we offend them, go to the sea, cast in a hook, and take the fish that comes up forth. And when you have opened its mouth, you will find a piece of money; take that and give it to them for Me and thee." – Matt 17:27

To honor rulers
"Let every soul be subject to the government authorities. For there is no authority except from God, and the authorities that exist are appointed by God." – Rom 13:1

To submit to government authority
"Submit yourselves to every ordinance of man." – I Pet 2:13

Duties of Rulers

Must be just
"The God of Israel said, The Rock of Israel spoke to me; 'He who rules over men must be just.' " – II Sam 23:3

Must be wise and serve God
"Now, therefore, be wise, O Kings; be instructed, you judges of the earth. Serve the Lord with fear." – Psa 2:10, 11

Consult Ezra 7:26; Eccles 8:2; Matt 27:21

Relationship Responsibilities

Duties to Aged Men

Hearken to them
"Listen to your father who begat you. And do not despise your mother when she is old." – Prov 23:22

Look to them as fathers
"Do not rebuke an older man, but exhort him as a father." – I Tim 5:1

Be exemplary
"The older men be sober, reverent, not slanderers, sound in faith, in love, in patience." – Tit 2:2

Duties of Young Men

Should be sober
"Exhort the young men to be sober-minded." – Tit 2:6

Should honor parents
"Honor your father and your mother." – Matt 15:4

Should obey parents
"Children obey your parents in the Lord, for this is right." – Eph 6:1

Duties of Women

Be keepers of the home
"(Young women) to be discreet, chaste, homemakers, good, obedient to heir own husbands, that the word of God be not blasphemed." - Titus 2:5

Be modest in dress
"Women adorn themselves in modest apparel." – I Tim 2:9

Cultivate inner spiritual life
"Do not let your beauty be that outward adorning of arranging the hair…but let it be the hidden person of the heart." – I Pet 3:3, 4

Duties of Masters

Should not threaten servants
"You masters…giving up threatenings, knowing that your own Master also is in heaven, and there is no partiality with Him." – Eph 6:9

Must be just in dealings
"Masters, give your servants what is just and fair, knowing that you also have a Master in heaven." – Col 4:1

Must be prompt in payment of wages
"Each day you should give him his wages, and let not the sun go down on it." – Deut 24:15

Duties of Servants

Should obey masters
"Servants, be obedient to those who are your masters." – Eph 6:5

Should be faithful
"Servants, obey in all things your masters according to the flesh, not with eye service, as men pleasers, but in sincerity of heart, fearing God." – Col 3:22

Should respect masters
"Let as many servants as are under the yoke count their own masters worthy of all honor, so that the name of God and His doctrine may not be blasphemed." – I Tim 6:1

Should desire to please
"Exhort servants to be obedient to their own masters, to be well pleasing in all things, not answering back." – Tit 2:9

Should be patient during hard times
"Servants, be submissive to your masters with all fear, not only to the good and gentle, but also to the harsh." – I Pet 2:18

Duties of Men

As Christian Brothers

To be impartial
"Love the stranger, for you were strangers in the land of Egypt." – Deut 10:19

To be sincere
"Let love be without hypocrisy." – Rom 12:9

To love one another
"May the Lord make you to increase and abound in love to one another and to all." – I Thess 3:12

As Citizens (See Civic Responsibilities)

As Employers (See Masters)

As Fathers (See Home Responsibilities)

As Husbands

To be faithful to wives
"Husbands, dwell with them with understanding, giving honor to the wife, as the weaker vessel." – I Pet 3:7

To love wives
"Husbands, love your wives, just as Christ also loved the church and gave Himself for it." – Eph 5:25

As Neighbors

To love them
"You shall love your neighbor as yourself." – Matt 19:19

To be unselfish
"You shall love your neighbor as yourself." – Matt 22:39

To try to please them
"Let each of us please his neighbor for his good, leading to edification."
– Rom 15:2

To Enemies

To love them
"I say to you, love your enemies, bless those who curse you." – Matt 5:44

To do them good
"I say to you, love your enemies, do good to them who hate you."
– Lk 6:27

To provide physical needs
"If your enemy hungers feed him; if he thirsts, give him drink." – Rom 12:20

To avoid retaliation
"See that no one renders evil for evil to anyone, but always pursue what is good for yourself and for all." – I Thess 5:15

To avoid trouble
"When you go with your adversary to the magistrate, make every effort along the way to settle with him." – Lk 12:58, 59

To avoid backbiting
"Do all things…for your edification…when I come I shall not find you such as I wish, and that I shall be found by you such as you do not wish; lest there be contentions, jealousies, outbursts of wrath, selfish ambitions, backbitings, whisperings, conceits, tumults."
– II Cor 12:19, 20

To Strangers

Manifest care for them
"The stranger who dwells among you shall be to you as one born among you, and you shall love him as yourself, for you were strangers in the land of Egypt." – Lev 19:34

Meet their physical needs
"I was hungry and you gave me food; I was thirsty and you gave me drink; I was a stranger and you took me in." – Matt 25:35

To the Weak

To supply their need
"We exhort you, brethren,…comfort the faint-hearted, uphold the weak."
– I Thess 5:14

To support them
"You must support the weak." – Acts 20:35

To bear their infirmities
"We then who are strong ought to bear with the scruples of the weak, and not to please ourselves." – Rom 15:1

To Widows and Fatherless
"Pure and undefiled religion before God and the Father is this; to visit orphans and widows in their trouble." – Jas 1:27

To Work

To be helpful to others
"Let him that stole steal no more, but rather let him labor, working with his hands, what is good, that he may have something to give to him who has need." – Eph 4:28

With quietness, earning our way
"We command and exhort through our Lord Jesus Christ that they work in quietness and eat their own bread." – II Thess 3:12

Labor for spiritual things also
"Do not labor for the food which perishes, but for the food which endures to everlasting life which the Son of Man will give you, because God the Father has set His seal on Him." – John 6:27

From this study it is apparent that a key word is "duty." To live fruitful Christian lives it is the duty of Christians to obey God and be dutiful in the practice of Christian virtues. This word also indicates that one's clarity of duty is involved in the successful operation of a total church program. Here is where job descriptions become important.